THREE PLAYS

THREE PLAYS

The Early Metaphysical Plays
of Charles Williams

By Charles Williams

WIPF & STOCK · Eugene, Oregon

Wipf and Stock Publishers
199 W 8th Ave, Suite 3
Eugene, OR 97401

Three Plays
The Early Metaphysical Plays of Charles Williams
By Williams, Charles
Copyright©1931 by Bruce Hunter/ CW Estate
ISBN 13: 978-1-60608-522-6
Publication date 8/11/2009
Previously published by Oxford Univ Press, 1931

Published in association with Watkins/Loomis Agency, Inc.
and David Higham Associates, Inc.

FOREWORD TO THE 2009 EDITION

How can Charles Williams be presented to anyone coming to his writing for the first time who does not know what to expect? Stripped of his linguistic difficulties, his work would doubtless be read widely and his name spoken in the same breath with G. K. Chesterton and C. S. Lewis, other Christian literary figures of the highest order. Twelve years younger than Chesterton, Williams contributed articles to G. K.'s Weekly; twelve years older than Lewis, Williams' thinking was the catalyst that sparked much of Lewis' full maturity as a thinker. Williams, however, lacked the firecracker popular wit of the older man. Nor did he possess the pellucid simplicity that marked the younger man's prose.

A third name needs introduction at this point. T. S. Eliot, about the same age as Williams, perfected modernist technique in English poetry, combining modern versification with French symbolist techniques to produce a fresh literary syntax capable of carrying the full weight of the complexity of late Western Civilization. The arbiters of taste in the 1920s thought him quite the rebel until his religious

FOREWORD

conversion; by this time, too many dictators of taste, what passed for critics in the English-speaking milieu of that time, had so extolled Eliot's virtues, so completely that not even Christianity could be held against him in the manner a la mode. Just as one cannot imagine Lewis' masterpiece, *That Hideous Strength*, without the thought of Williams lurking somewhere in the background, so too, the much lauded *Four Quartets* owe much of its intellectual power to ideas Eliot found in Williams' theological insights, "At the still point of the turning world."

Add to these writers one continuing tradition of British religious poetry, which was also the context of Williams' intellectual development, and his historical context is complete—belonging to the school of such strong versifiers as Coventry Patmore, Gerard Manley Hopkins, Francis Thompson, and even Ernest Dowson. Here is catholic content replete with vigorous and intense late romantic imagery—qualities not in Eliot or Lewis, not even in Chesterton, whose poetry owes more to the ballad tradition than to that of the world of a baptized Keats. The dominant tone of the British catholic (Roman or Anglo-) from about 1870–1930 was, paradoxically, baroque and terse at once, highly polished but with the feel of the roughhewn, while fusing hard theology with heart-moving melody.

Williams' best work effortlessly melds all these disparate elements into a single whole. Though a major achievement, his extreme condensation of language that couples with a specialized vocabulary necessary to his content has resulted

FOREWORD

in Williams' audience being much smaller than he deserves. Almost no matter what he writes, he enters into his subject from some angle foreign to the presuppositions current in our age.

Thus his Christianity will be off-putting to some, but even Dante (about whom Williams wrote arguably the finest critical study) troubles such people. Many of those most sympathetic to his content find his manner unusual, eccentric to the point of constituting a distraction. If he is worth reading and his work endures, it will only come about with a revival of the modes of thought and manner of the writers who form the matrix of his world *and* his presentation: Chesterton, Lewis, Eliot, and what can be called the school of Hopkins. (Another direct connection: Williams was Hopkins' first professional editor.)

Yet a sizable enough minority has kept his name alive and his books read—and a number of these readers, the present essayist included, do not find him the least bit difficult to read, but that is largely because we share his assumptions. What then are the real obstacles to appreciating what he has to say? First, each sentence he writes tells and is built, even founded, on the preceding one, creating an extremely dense prose and an even more compact poetry. He comes to his style as parcel of what he is saying and always in the manner, if not in the presentation, of a poet. Not only that, his highly idiosyncratic vocabulary, which he sometimes neglects to define, often does not meet the reader halfway; he must surrender to Williams' vision or get nothing from

FOREWORD

the his text. Yet Williams does not scorn his readership by deliberate obscurity. Rather his insights, which flow inevitably from his habitual vision, demands special attention to communicate his ideas on *any* level. This can bewilder, and many encountering Williams come away bewildered.

• • •

Three Plays was his first dramatic writing for public consumption. Published in 1931, no one has performed any of them publicly to my knowledge. Williams had written some masques earlier, but these were for production among members of his set at Oxford University Press where he earned his living as an editor. The masques, however, have held up so well that they too have been reprinted in recent years. Yet the three plays of the title, although superior work to the private dramas, have wallowed in total obscurity for close to eighty years and copies are exceedingly rare, so rare that only perhaps one hundred or so libraries own one, and $183.00 was the cheapest listed price for purchase on the Internet in July, 2008.

I can imagine no one with a higher opinion than I have of John Heath-Stubbs, who wrote probably the best long poem in English in the twentieth century, *Artorius*, although Chesterton's *The Ballad of the White Horse* makes it a close race. He was also the editor of Williams' *Collected Plays*, but he somehow managed not to collect these three, wrongly thinking them unworthy. Although none is equal to *Thomas Cranmer of Canterbury* or *The House of the Octopus*, surely

This 2009 edition is dedicated to the

Charles Williams Society

FOREWORD

they surpass the vast majority of plays written in the language in the past eight decades. Heath-Stubbs fell short of his task by the exact number of three. This volume rectifies that problem.

THE POEMS

Williams intersperses five poems not connected to the plays throughout the book, and they are something of a trial run for what will become the Taliessin cycle. No reason is offered for their inclusion, but any otherwise unavailable poetry of Williams is well worth reprinting. Although not of the towering level of anything in *Taliessin Through Logres* or *The Region of the Summer Stars*, they are excellent of their kind and might have provided fitting interludes had Williams lived long enough to organize and complete the Arthurian poems. Lines like these should not be consigned to the wastepaper basket:

> In the City of the Caesars at the Emperor's feet I fell,
> and prayed by his providence bring Logres forth from hell
> from the years of devastation, from the famine and the toil
> in cities and in cornland become the pirates' spoil.

Even if the plays were worthless, this project would be well worth the effort simply to save these poems. But the plays are not worthless.

FOREWORD

THE WITCH

The Witch should hold pride of place as the archetype of the post-World War I English Christian verse drama. Eliot, Dorothy L. Sayers, Christopher Fry, Williams himself—this is a truly impressive list of playwrights considering that they wrote in a genre the zeitgeist found uncongenial to its whims and in an atmosphere it positively detested, because it found all Christianity repugnant.

So much the worse for the zeitgeist. Any canon that includes Virginia Woolf and ignores Hilaire Belloc should be shunned like arsenic and with the bemused smile that so ridiculous a standard could possibly be taken seriously by anyone who can read.

The Witch images the Parable of the Vineyard (Luke 20:13–15), especially the title character in the role of the tenants. Bess, who desires the destruction of her landlord against whom she bears a grudge, is ". . . a poor old crone/ [Who w]ith rheumatic finger on their throats/Fingers their windpipes."

She desires her daughter, the inconstant Rhoda, to entice the squire's son, Gerald—which enticement Rhoda wishes in any case. Gerald is a poet with the personality of a lovesick puppy—ever a bad combination. His poetical master is, tellingly, Shelley, whom death seemed to shadow, and who brought destruction to those closest to him.

Inevitably, Rhoda and Gerald proclaim their love, while Bess reiterates her wish to destroy the squire. With intrigu-

FOREWORD

ing complications, such as Bess harboring her son, an escaped criminal, the dramatic action reaches its apex with the attempts of the squire's bailiff to elope with the fickle Rhoda, resulting in tragedy. Bess not only gets the last word, she declares the point of the tale which, translated into cold prose is that original sin, not any spells, caused these actions. Thus the world of *The Witch* is akin to that of Greek tragedy, where the chorus shouts, "Fate, fate" just as the characters affirm free will. Williams, in philosophy, was a Scotist, as he stated in a private letter. This play demonstrates that even in tragedy wounded souls uphold free will in what Williams calls the Coinherence.

THE CHASTE WANTON

Whereas *The Witch* would hold the stage and prefigures such well-known dramas as The *Lady's Not for Burning* and *The Zeal of thy House*, *The Chaste Wanton* is a chamber-drama. Had radio theatre survived the advent of television, this play could have, with appropriate dissemination, secured a similar audience to that of *Under Milk Wood* and *The Man Born to Be King*.

We meet a dowager duchess wondering whom she will marry. Various figures assert a complete range of opinion concerning the nature of love. For her uncle, the bishop, love is primarily temperance, while for one of the ladies, it is burning passion, and for another character love is intellectual fire. Nearly every commonly accepted viewpoint on the subject receives a champion and the duchess resides

FOREWORD

over an inconclusive formal disputation on the matter. The primary action focuses on the events intended to culminate in the duchess' marriage, symbolically the survival of the duchy and its people—that which secures a happy life. She is a virgin—but one who tempts all who meet her. Thus the title; she is a "chaste wanton," and her very being is a mirror reflecting whatever prejudices others bring to her. This is the gift of all successful politicians no matter what the system.

Then an alchemical master, Vincenzo, arrives at court. "All is significant that undergoes process and transmutation" observes one character. The duchess and Vincenzo discuss the matter:

> Duchess: But to know God—and is there a God to know?
>
> Vincenzo: Ask if there is aught else, Highness, but to know?

Thus God is in all and all is in God. This is a variation of Williams' oft-repeated concept: "This also is Thou; neither is this Thou." Both affirming and denying the images of God which are necessary facets of a fully human life.

How does this play out in the world? To speak more would take us into the heart of mystical theology and would require at least several tomes. Let it be said that Williams provides in dramatic dialogue a wholly satisfactory answer to the question of Love; that Love is the principle basis of Being. And note the personification. The only place left

FOREWORD

for Williams to go is to the third play, from the hell of *The Witch*, to the purgatory of *The Chaste Wanton*, to the heaven of *The Rites of the Passion*. Passion as heaven is another in the endless paradoxes central to these plays.

THE RITES OF THE PASSION

Intended to be performed in church, anticipating *Murder in the Cathedral* by over half a decade, Williams' play is a liturgical celebration, bringing the audience back to the medieval rites from which modern drama sprang. Williams embeds seven familiar hymns of the Church of England into his text, making this work a de facto collaboration with major hymnodists of the faith.

Even were we to observe that pageant predominates over dramatic action in this piece, yet one can imagine what it would gain in performance, for example the tension created by the relative positioning onstage of such antithetical characters as Satan and Gabriel in their contentions, and all counterpointed by the singing of a minstrel offering his gift of song to God:

> The Child upon Our Lady's lap
> the kings bowed down before
> to see this wonder, by good hap,
> the slaves thronged at the door.

Peter, James, John, Mary, the voice of Love (the Holy Ghost) celebrate Love born as Christ and come to maturity at Cana in response to Mary's "They have no wine," here a metaphor

FOREWORD

of the state of humanity before the incarnation. This is almost liturgy that a John Donne might conceive.

From this point forth, Love is identified as the Christ and will lead to his Passion: "Lo I who once did your young beauty bless/now go upon my Father's business/into your clamorous marketplace of sin."

Thus we proceed until the Redeemer sanctifies all. Poetry, drama, theology. In Williams they coalesce, nay, they converge. This also is Thou; neither is this Thou.

Arthur Livingston
September 2008
Chicago, Illinois

NOTE

Two of these plays are occasional; the other is, in a sense, accidental. *The Witch* was written as a play in verse for eight persons at the request of Mr. Frank Geary, Principal of the Balham Commercial Institute. Having said this, I am required by a regulation of the London County Council to say that the Council accept no responsibility for any opinions expressed in the book, and this, with great pleasure, I hasten to do.

The title *The Chaste Wanton* is due, I believe, to Mr. Gerard Hopkins, who dropped it casually in conversation as possible for a mock-Elizabethan play. But, before the amusement was begun, it or I had turned serious, and the title enlarged its meaning beyond its original scope. I feel it is only right to add that Mr. Hopkins also has no responsibility for any opinions expressed in the book, or for the solemnity with which his remark has been invested by a duller mind than his own.

The Rite of the Passion was written at the request of the Rev. A. H. E. Lee, Vicar of St. Martin's, Kensal Rise, for the Three Hours Service at that church on Good Friday, 1929, when it was read with intervals of prayer, meditation, and music. I permitted myself to include in it a few poems which have appeared in others of my books. The hymns sung are given (as a matter of interest) in a short list at the end. Mr. Lee is officially bound and is personally willing to accept more responsibility than are my other co-authors for the statements made here. I can only hope he is justified.

All three pieces, however, though separate in origin

NOTE

and manner, are from a certain point of view in relation to each other. They form a progression, and it is to accentuate this that I have enclosed them between poems which deal with the same progression under colour of one of the great English myths. The Taliessin poems are from an attempted and unfinished cycle, of which a part appeared in *Heroes and Kings*, which proposed to begin with the distress of Logres, to speak of the vision of the elect soul, of the establishment of Arthur, of the transmutation of the Table at the coming of the High Prince, and of his achievement. Outside which (as some tell us) man has no concern.

It is true that this concern does not necessarily make the poetry interesting; sanctity too often amuses herself with her poor relations.

CONTENTS

	PAGE
Taliessin's Song of Logres	1
THE WITCH	5
Taliessin's Song of Byzantion	65
THE CHASTE WANTON	69
Taliessin's Song of the King's Crowning	135
THE RITE OF THE PASSION	139
Taliessin's Song of the Setting of Galahad in the King's Bed	193
Epilogue in Somerset: A Song of the Myths	197

TALIESSIN'S SONG OF LOGRES

Logres lieth with sorrow riven—
   how shall the lord of salvation come?—
to the wolves, the pagans, the pirates given,
   to the hordes and the galleys of heathendom.
From the rocky hills and the roaring sea
the kings come down and our people flee.
   When shall the lord of salvation draw
armies after him? till we know
   peace that springeth from tables of law,
Logres waileth in desolate woe.

Uther Pendragon is king no more;
   lieth he deep in a royal tomb.
O but the robbers from shore to shore
   ride and ravage and sit in his room.
As wind, as thunder, as fire, they go;
Logres waileth in desolate woe.
   They ride in the place of a throne unmade,
they roar and crash in a shaken sky
   as the planets roared ere their path was stayed,
and the world was ordered, in peace to fly.

All the fierceness that ruled of yore
   is come again upon Logres strand,
King Brandegoris of Strangore,
   King Clariance of Northumberland;
King Urience over his plunder smiles;
King Lot of Orkney and all the isles
   hath sworn a league with King Agwisaunce
to send their ships on the little ports;
   on the inland towns with an evil lance
King Idras rides from his southern forts.

TALIESSIN'S SONG OF LOGRES

The nameless king of the hundred knights
   hath burned the castle of Terrabil;
King Cradlemas worketh his bloody rites
   in the city of Camelot at his will;
no word from Byzantion is come,
where the Emperor sitteth blind and dumb;
   in his hall of Benwick the good King Ban
is shut by Duke Cambenet's tyranny;
   from Brittany King Leodogran
dare not adventure over sea.

The wolves run wild in the snowy woods,
   as the hounds of Satan they run and howl;
no man hath surety of life or goods
   nor maiden safety, but all goes foul;
and the Roman sits in Byzantion,
no help comes down from the Sacred Throne,
   but the lords of chaos go roaring by,
and creation ruins where'er they go,
   order is lost in earth and sky,
Logres lieth in desolate woe.

Loosed are the powers of earth and air,
   fire and water in combat leap;
space is now but a broken stair,
   and the great sun runs on the edge of a steep
dizzy with terror; for all around
the elementals again abound
   in clamour and freedom; water, fire,
earth and air unprison their powers,
   and no prayer reacheth the heavenly Sire
where he sitteth calm in his lucid towers.

TALIESSIN'S SONG OF LOGRES

Myriad atoms of man and beast
    strive apart as the kingdom strives;
within and without hath concord ceased
    for terror striketh the least of lives;
the summer gnat in his flight upsprings
for rage of the torment that takes his wings,
    the wolves for hunger but more for pain
 howl and ravin about the moors,
    chaos is come upon earth again
and the pirates drive upon Logres' shores.

Dubric the Shepherd lieth hid
    in cellars of Cantuar and its towns,
Winchester keepeth its Bishop amid
    huts and copses of southward downs;
but I will go, as one goeth far
to the saint that sits by the morning star,
    over the sea and the land of Gaul
to the house of the Emperor's majesty
    to view if such evil there befall
or whether some help upon earth may be.

The popes and patriarchs watch with him,
    sitting around him on golden thrones,
studying sayings of cherubim
    or adepts ranked in celestial zones;
there in a mitre and woven robe
sitteth the Master of all the globe—
    consuls and tribunes before his feet
bear their part in the rule of man,
    and the camel-drivers in the street
unload the tribute of Ispahan.

TALIESSIN'S SONG OF LOGRES

I, Taliessin, a goddess' son,
    nurtured the round Welsh hills among,
who also have not unwisely done
    in courts of music and schools of song,
I will take ship for the Sacred Throne
and there will I make one verse alone,
    one lament for the world that falls,
one cry for help ere the worst is done,
    I will send it shrill through the Emperor's halls:
This will I do in Byzantion.

For Logres is fallen, is fallen at last
    into a doom no heart can stay,
now champion and warrior flee aghast,
    no prefect rides up the Roman way.
Uther is dead, Pendragon is dead,
the soul of man is a leaf that is shed
    on storms of winter; I hear its wail
perish in darkness, wherefore I go
    to see if lordship can still prevail.
Logres lieth in desolate woe.

THE WITCH

The action takes place in a village of the West country some time early in the nineteenth century. The scene is outside a ruinous cottage on the edge of a common: a neglected road runs before it; beyond is the open country.

ACT I

[Evening. ANNE comes in.]

ANNE [knocking]: Bess! Bess! art there? 'tis I, 'tis Anne
  that calls.
BESS [at the door]: None other, I warrant me; none other comes
  to see the outcast, the old crone, the witch.
ANNE: Fair fall them then and you! Good cheer, old Bess;
  here is butter, here are eggs, my husband bade
  bring hither when time served the walk.
BESS: For this
  your sow shall run unharmed this breeding time.
ANNE: That's as may be; our thanks for the goodwill.
BESS: There's no goodwill in me nor in the folk
  that point thumbs after me behind a hedge;
  aye, and curse under breath and then aloud
  when all their curses do not save their hens
  from laying addled eggs or none at all.
ANNE: God a mercy, Bess, and would you curse their hens
  because a dozen women cackle more
  than all the hens God's mercy ever made?
  Who cares for what a flock of hens can do,
  perching and perking and scrabbling in the dirt?
BESS: Why, so—to see them flap and scurry aside
  and all in a flurry drive their chickens home
  when I go peeping by the lane's corner.
ANNE: Chut!
  You like to see them run?
BESS: And others than they
  skirr when the witch looks out of doors at the world.
ANNE: What pleasure to see men's faces fall awry,

    or such a girl's heart as your Rhoda's beat
    with fear of her sweetheart dying from no pain
    but that same lingering fever in his breast
    as melting wax—to those that dread it—brings?
BESS: Ah Anne, well-to-do Anne, farm-owning Anne,
    you have not lain abed December nights,
    cold more than needs for but one blanket's need,
    snow in the chimney, and no food to hand,
    yet warm as a fox in his burrow just to know
    that some strong man, some man much like your Giles,
    lay shivering all the night, with blankets enow
    to keep his feet warm, but no warmth at heart,
    for just a little snick of fear within,
    lest you should hate him—
ANNE: Giles would never fear!—
BESS: or his wife or babies, comfortable Anne.
    And there's a rich man too, there's the squire's self,
    'twixt fear and anger sleeps but little of nights.
    That keeps me warmer than the great log fire
    piled in his hall when first October blows.
ANNE: But what's your gain, Bess, if they fear you so?
BESS: Just to lie there and know a poor old crone,
    with her rheumatic finger on their throats,
    fingers their windpipes; so they draw deep breaths,
    cursing her curses, but they doze with dreams . . .
    Anne, have you ever watched your Giles asleep?
ANNE: God a mercy, Bess, I sleep as sound as he;
    no time to sit and watch him in the day,
    less time to lie and watch him in the night.
    Besides, all's under God.
BESS: Aye, and strange things
    go running abroad in the moonlight under him.

THE WITCH

He has watched a million moons out, and not stooped
to check one weaselly red-bellied shape,
that might be vermin and might be something else,
loosed from a witch's door when clocks strike twelve.

ANNE: It's living alone and looking at the moon
that makes you think so. Rhoda's just a girl.
Come over this winter and share a room with us,
I'll warrant you see no vermin.

BESS: And be warm,
and fed, and cossetted—and not a smile
to be struck off a face when I come in,
but the squire to give me cloth and take the land.
If I was out, he'd quick enough be in—
this strip that parts him from the common land
and keeps his wall from going where it will.
Fine straying walls squires have, like straying mares,
to go all over the world and come back home,
when they have eaten their fill of others' grass.
I block him here, and bitter he finds it too.
Black witchcraft isn't only in the poor.

ANNE: There's few that say so. How does your Rhoda
     keep?

BESS: O finely, finely, going about the world.
She's got her longing, and shall find it out.
I know.

ANNE: And will you help to give it her?

BESS: There's something here in me that rules the world
from dawn to sunset; farm and village and town
lurk watching for it, and when once it comes
it helps them out to get what they desire.
Witchcraft or devilry or fate: there's craft
to rule the lazy kingdoms of the world

or get a child the heart of her desire,
and I will get it her, before the years
have puzzled men three times with hate and fear.
ANNE: Bess, don't you think too much of hate and fear
and hunger? Hunger never filled itself,
and odd things come with thinking of odd things.
BESS: It's no odd thing she needs. Look.
ANNE: What, she walks
with the squire's agent then?
BESS: None such for her;
I sang a catch with a black-horned goat one night
to see what he would tell me, and he sang—
Youth, riches, knighthood—a thrice-tangled tale.
ANNE: Well, I don't love Ralph Carter near enough
to stop and meet him.
BESS: Fear him then, wise Anne?
ANNE: Fear him? I fear him? there's no rent been owed,
quarter by quarter, since we held the farm.
I'd fear you sooner.
BESS: Wisely said; your sow
shall surely run unharmed and get its young,
nor shall Giles break his leg when mending roofs.
Husband and sow safe, will you long for more?
[ANNE goes out with something like a snort, as RALPH CARTER and
RHODA come in]
RHODA: Mother, here's Mr. Carter, with a word
to say to you yourself.
BESS: A word for me?
Bless us, a word—vixen or harridan,
old bitch—that's two; one from the squire, and one
from Mr. Carter's sweet good-languaged self.
He hasn't got his master's tongue—nor I

Act I   THE WITCH

    an ear to hear a serving-man's abuse,
    save what a flick to my little Malkin boy
    may set him on to answer. Malkin's the lad
    to steal by night and suck fat servants' blood;
    ease them, and save them physic. Well, the word?
CARTER: Ha, ha! Why, old Bess, you've a proper tongue
    to tease the squire's friends.—Don't go, Rhoda.
BESS: No,
    Rhoda; don't go; the squire's man bids you stay.
    Curtsey to thank him. If you were a lady, child,
    and had a footman for your coach, d'you think
    he'd be too plump and lazy?
CARTER: Look you, Bess,
    I give you license—
BESS: Step inside, and see
    if there's a rabbit hanging in the smoke,
    trapped . . . trapped . . . trapped . . . so.
CARTER: You don't snare rabbits, Bess.
BESS: No? I've got something trapped hanging inside;
    the squire's pet thought—a bouncing baby, trapped.
    Wishes grow fat, and when they can't grow deeds,
    the old witch keeps them dangling in her shed.
    It's growing plump with longing now, that wish
    the squire bred in his brain for me to snare.
    Wishes go bad when they've been kept too long.
RHODA: Let's hear him, mother.
CARTER: Rhoda, you're a lass
    that knows where profit lies.
BESS: Not yet, not quite.
    It takes more talk than Rhoda's ever had
    by nights with little Malkin, or his sire,
    my master, the tall black who sent him here.

CARTER: Rhoda, I told you I'd a word to say
that might do good to all. This hut's too old
for any Christian soul. Now up the hill
there's a new cottage with two rooms. The squire
offers your mother this in change for hers.
BESS: And the land this stands on?
CARTER: Ten pounds for the land;
ten pounds, and a cottage twice as good as this.
BESS: And then the squire's wall could go straying out
just where his ugly nightmare runs each night,
and graze on the common. Should I sleep so warm?
CARTER: Warm?
BESS: Aye, with joy to know the squire can't sleep.
O aye, I've got his baby hanging up,
his wish, his wish. And if he had this hut,
he'd get his precious baby back again.
It goes with the hut, my clever serving-man.
RHODA: Mother—
BESS: Be quiet, child.
CARTER: Aye, be quiet, child. Bess,
it's well to hush her. She might wish for room
to stretch an arm in and not strike the wall
unless the broken window let it through.
Rhoda, I thought of you the whole long while
I quarrelled with the squire to make the change.
And here's your mother quarrelling with you,
only for fear that you might want the change.
Well, take it as you will. I meant my best.
BESS: Rhoda's your best? better than all your best,
and meat for your betters, serving-man. Go back
and tell your master I'm too old to lose
the land and the hut and the baby in the smoke;

Act I THE WITCH

the baby that gets fat as he gets lean.
CARTER: Rhoda?
BESS: No word.
RHODA: Mother—
BESS: No word. I know
what Malkin means to come, and what I mean.
CARTER: What's Malkin then to keep you here?
BESS: My chuck,
my sweet boy, my dear imp, my little black
bad-hearted agile fancy; he that sits
couched on my shoulder or my knee, and sings
of what he runs about the world to do,
drop sparks, lame cows, or whisper in the ear
of squires nigh sick for walls that can't get out
over the common. Little Malkin sweet!
CARTER: If you should talk so to a justice, witch—
BESS: Isn't the squire a justice?
CARTER: If he heard
Bedlam might take you, and the whips and chains
kept for such maniacs as believe they talk
with such an imp of the devil under the moon.
RHODA: Ah!
CARTER: Nay, forgive me, child; it is her way.
What pleasure she finds in it I cannot tell
and would not grudge her, but to keep you close
in this half-hut, half-sty—that maddens me.
Forgive me; I must needs be jealous for you
who are too mild to be so for yourself.
Here's the squire coming.
BESS: Squire and justice too,
and cock o' the village on all hearths but here.
        [The SQUIRE comes in]

CARTER [to him]: I've told her; she won't bite. Try if it tastes
  sweeter from yours the master's hand, than mine.
SQUIRE: Well, Bess, have you heard my offer? Come, be wise.
  Think on your children.
BESS: Ah that's what I do,
  evening and morning. Would they prosper, squire—
  or would she prosper that's the only one
  left here to tell me what love meant? They say
  she favours her father—a fine figure, squire.
SQUIRE: Yes, it's a hard thing to be left alone.
BESS: Don't we both know it? Why, your lady, squire,
  she would have been now just my husband's age.
SQUIRE: Not by a score of years; and see you, Bess,
  don't lick my wife's name with your tongue.
BESS: Why, no.
  She *was* a lady, wasn't she? Not like
  farm-maids or witches or women of the town.
SQUIRE: Keep your mouth shut.
CARTER: Gently, go gently, sir,
  or she'll refuse you just to thwart your will.
BESS: Why now, what harm in a gay lady's life?
  'Tisn't for us who are moral, being poor—
  Rhoda and me: *her* honesty's her trade;
  but you and your boy I warrant have known a mort
  of women to drink with and slip bodices down.
  Isn't a college town a likely place
  for come-by-nights to play in?
SQUIRE: God's my life!
  You—get out, Carter!—you black beldame! you!
  you'd foul my son's name? you'd twitch tales of him?

Act I   THE WITCH

where's your own? hanged in London now belike,
as you shall be—or burned for witchcraft!
BESS: Me
for witchcraft? there was a jovial squire once burned
a witch for her craft—she was a witch with power—
and on the year's mind of her death it fell
his son was borne to Bedlam, and his goods
and lands all went to ruin for want of an heir.
Witches don't only work while they're alive;
but leave the spiders in the manor house
to sit by a young heir's pillow and spin him dreams
out of their bellies, till his brain's no more
than a fat spider's belly of sticky web.
SQUIRE: God curse you!
BESS: Ah God's like to listen to you;
He never listens to a wish; that's why
all who wish strongly have to slip and find
the black man who sends Malkin. Farewell, squire.
Go back to your gay London dame my son
whistled in London, ere she liked your gold.
                           [*She goes into the hut*
CARTER [*leaving* RHODA, *with whom he has been whispering from time to time*]: You've lost her?
SQUIRE: Damn her, she'll lose home and life.
I'll draw a warrant—
CARTER: Better not.
SQUIRE: Why not?
I tell you she shan't bully me for naught.
She'll rue it.
CARTER: Better not.
SQUIRE: Why, you don't think
there's anything in her talk?

CARTER: I think wise men
don't put out poison on the supper board
when their sons come from Oxford. Go you home
and quiet yourself to meet him there. I'll come
after a word with the girl.
SQUIRE: I won't believe
in all this devil's work—God keep us safe!
why don't the village try her in the pond
or stone her all at once with none to blame?
CARTER: And that may come, but keep you far enough.
Get back, or Gerald will be home ere you,
and pacing up and down the terrace stones
and quoting poetry softly to himself,
quite out of heart with you and all you want
to talk of with him; yes, and you must needs
go softly with your visitor at the house.
SQUIRE: That's not his business.
CARTER: Lest he make it so,
be early there to talk with him. See you,
I know your son—he's all in love with words;
anything's right so long as it's finely said.
SQUIRE: I can't talk finely.
CARTER: Talk to him of yourself;
he'll make the fineness. Why, the commonest maid
talking to him in twilight here would touch
his young heart into ecstasy, and her words
make of his ear a tiring room to come
thence like play-acting queens into his brain.
Be quiet, be simple. Get you home to him.
I'll follow.
SQUIRE: Carter, if she died the house—
CARTER: 'Tchut. If she died, the house would drop apart

Act I   THE WITCH

with wind and rain. Leave it at that.
SQUIRE: You'll come?
CARTER: At once. No warrants till I've tried the girl.
                               [The SQUIRE goes out
Kiss me; it's dark enough.   [RHODA kisses him
Why I stay here!— and why you make me stay!—
Fine buffers for two lunatics to bruise!
The squire's least mad, he's crazy for the land,
but what your mother's crazy for none knows.
RHODA: That's where she's strong; I think none knows
    her will;
perhaps she has no will except her will.
Ralph, I could once have been as strong as she
if . . .
CARTER: If?
RHODA: Don't make me say it.
CARTER: No excuse;
    out with it.
RHODA: If you—isn't that enough?
The witch's daughter to be just a girl
because a man is stronger!
CARTER: Ah that's it,
    isn't it, Rhoda?
RHODA: If my mother knew!
BESS [from the hut]: Rhoda!
CARTER: She doesn't. Come away with me.
    Why must we stay?
RHODA: I know . . . but, Ralph, to feel
myself in London and no guard but you;
no rock but you to build on! It's too sweet,
too terrible with sweetness; let me taste
a little longer.

CARTER: What, still frightened?
RHODA: Just to look at being frightened—
BESS: Rhoda!
RHODA: Hark, I can't stay now. Besides, Ralph, you've known girls—
you know they like to feel themselves pressed on,
still holding fast: but once let go, one arm
only to cling to—that's a different joy.
I wouldn't change this joy for that too soon.
CARTER: Whimsies! If you'd known men as I've known girls
you'd know the pleasure was in being loved,
not thinking about it.
RHODA: If I'd been the first!
CARTER: The first or one-and-twentieth, all's the same.
I bet you've kissed a farm-hand—every way,
for all I care; I don't begrudge it. Love's
as fresh as ever if the heart's as good
and the will in it.
BESS: Rhoda!
RHODA: I must go;
good-night. She's coming. Good-night; go. Good-night.
[*He kisses her and goes.* BESS *comes from the hut.*]
Did you want me, mother?
BESS: Naught but to stay here.
One's coming worth our pains.
RHODA: Who? the squire's son?
BESS: Stay so, and bless the moon for shining out.
He'll come this way.
RHODA: Why must I talk to him?

Act I   THE WITCH

BESS: Because the moon and you and clever talk
  will maze what brains he's got, and then he's yours.
  You'll waste time with the servant; here's the heir.
RHODA: He won't dare wed me!
BESS: Wait till his father knows.
  I've watched them years; a pretty boy; he went
  dreaming, and dreams still. Oxford's near by night,
  and Malkin knows him or I know him there.
  Show him his dreams; talk little but talk well.
RHODA: But what do we catch if we should catch the heir?
BESS: I'd go to hell to see the squire gone dazed
  to know the witch's daughter got with child—
  or let him think so; there are herbs to turn
  seed into barrenness. And then the gold
  he'll offer and we'll spill! O Rhoda girl,
  the game's beginning. Hark, he's coming; back
  a little into the hut; then out, and wait.
                       [*They move into the hut door*
GERALD [*without*]: Good-night; good-night. 'A fair
   good-night to all.'   [*He comes in*
Well rid of you, good fellows! I have dreamed
a thousand years in this half-hour, and felt
the clouds quench all the catches. This is night,
being the solitude wherein the mind
considers its own beauty, dark and full
and far from the rough noises of the world,
so that a friend's voice is intrusion; yes,
not even the sacred poets yet have found
a name for the only voice that Silence owns—
unless that god the Mediterranean drowned
were it, unless our master Shelley were it,
marvellous, aboriginal, divine.

If such a voice should sound now, if this night
and silence and the whole invisible mind
of the dark universe should speak some word
simple as its own nature; it might be,
if deafness did not clog our mortal ears.
BESS [at the door to RHODA]: All's yours now; speak to
him. He's yet too young
to know if speech like yours be false or true.
He hears the voice and not the accent—go.
RHODA: Sir, did you want my mother?
GERALD: I?
RHODA: I thought
you looked ... forgive me.
GERALD: This is more than chance;
this is the longing of all loveliness
to find a voice. Who is your mother, child?
RHODA: She lives here, in this hut. I thought you came
to find her.
GERALD: Child, your mother was the moon
immaculately conceiving in some dark
valley of Latmos the inconceivable
Beauty's most holy incarnation. Say,
have you not heard—has not a rumour spread
you are the very daughter of the moon?
RHODA: O not the moon, but one that knows the moon.
I am the child of a wise woman, born,
certainly, when the moon was very high
on a March evening.
GERALD: No—you are the Spring,
you are Persephone, maiden and queen,
at the winter solstice turning from the dark.
Stand still, and let me play with dreams of you.

Act I   THE WITCH

I will not hear your name.
RHODA: Perhaps indeed
I have no true name, for my mother says
our true names are enchantment and not known,
or if known never to be sounded forth
among the uninstructed.
GERALD: O wise maid,
I have spent years in Oxford but to taste
antique philosophies springing from that root.
Will you be found as wise as Oxford seems?
RHODA: I have no wisdom, but my mother says
no man can utterly have power on us
unless he call us by our hidden names.
GERALD: Tell me your name then; tell me your hidden name.
RHODA: Why, would you utterly have power on me?
GERALD: I would have power on you or you on me.
It is a perilous thing to meet by night
upon these heaths a more than mortal maid
and talk with her, unless there is a strength
to pass unhurt and leave her. No mere song
brought Orpheus past the Sirens, but their names
cried o'er the ocean drew them to their doom;
it was the strife of Pan to speak the name
of our Chief Master that made black the sun,
and when the god's mouth failed upon the large
syllables of that Tetragrammaton,
all nature moaned, crying that Pan was dead.
And I would bind you, whether you be maid,
fairy, or goddess, or what other shape
of fabulous imagination now
my mind mistakes you for, with such iron spells

as the adepts once in Eleusis knew
to prop the portcullis of the underworld.
RHODA: Whether I were a goddess or a maid
you should not hold me but by other bands.
GERALD: O but the stronger hold the weaker bands;
Cynthia, consider all things are within,
nor think that when you, with a holy kiss,
first wooed your brother, chaste Endymion,
into the clear virginity of love,
his sleep knew other than your very self
breathed over him in your significant name.
RHODA: I do not know these names.
GERALD: They are your past,
but you are willing to forget them now.
And be content to lose them. Do you know
that he you speak to is a mortal man,
or do you dream that you are still afar
among the immortal gods in Thessaly?
RHODA: I know the farmers and the farmers' boys,
but beyond these I know my mother tells
of other meetings where the tribe of the air
mingle at midnight with such human folk
as ride upon strange horses to the feast.
GERALD: What is your mother?
RHODA: A wise woman.
GERALD: Wise
indeed if she can know the ancient things;
and what are you? Tell me your worldly name.
RHODA: My name is Rhoda—
GERALD: Ay, I had forgot.
You are the daughter of old Bess the witch—
RHODA: Will you too speak of her as farmers do?

Act I   THE WITCH

GERALD: You have forgotten me; you never saw
a boy look at you from behind a hedge
as boys will at such beauty as they feel
bears them into a rapture out of time.
I know you, Rhoda; when I was a boy,
being forbidden to pass by this way
lest your wise mother should put spells on me,
I stopped here once and saw you.
RHODA: At that hour
I think you came for ever to my dreams,
but then I never dreamed that you would make
a jest of me, as all this while you do.
GERALD: I jest?
RHODA: Call me a goddess, fairy-born,
moon-nurtured. You have shamed me.
GERALD: Never that.
Being mortal, you are even more divine
than if you were mere goddess. O your hand
has meaning in it more than deities have
when they unclothe their being of its cloud.
Rhoda, it is not I can scorn or shame;
do not forget me, do not go from me.
RHODA: You are the squire's son, and I am the child
of a wise woman; loose me, let me go.
GERALD: Your face is like the Oxford halls by night
seen from some neighbouring hill where poets dwell,
or like a page of Hebrew charms—so full
are they of meaning; were you all they meant?
RHODA: Leave me, I cannot bear it, let me dream.
GERALD: No dreaming—all significant and full
of purpose. Rhoda, can the squire's son dare
hold these hands fast? these that have made the world,

and are the origin of space and time?
Sweet, can I let you go?
RHODA: You must, you must;
I am not meant for you—I—O let go;
To-morrow, if you will.
GERALD: To-morrow? no,
this is to-morrow; only in your eyes
the future sits—if I should part from you
I should go out of the universe; God made
nothing but you, and outside you and Him
there is eternal nothingness and void.
RHODA: But I—you said—am a wise woman's child
and know there is to-morrow. Let me go;
come if you will and see my face by day,
and then perhaps you will not grieve to know
I and to-morrow need no more be one.
GERALD: A challenge?
RHODA: Yes, a challenge—go your way.
A challenge—till to-morrow.
GERALD: Undo then
this spell with other spells. [He kisses her.] No challenge; naught
but the most inward silence of the night.
[He looks at her and goes. When he is out of hearing RHODA turns to her mother]
RHODA: I think he'll come to-morrow.
BESS [from the door]: O he'll come.
I have a way of knowing; keep your talk
simple and innocent and yet sounding wise.
But he'll believe you wise, whether or no,
being drunk with youth and beauty and his dreams.
RHODA: And when he comes?

Act I   THE WITCH

BESS: I find a way to pull
the squire to ruin or you to the squire's chair,
and either way the squire will fret to death,
and round his bed will my black lord and I
foot a gay ghostly dance that he shall see
but not the doctor nor the maids. O rare!
If you shall know him sick and see me squat
very still in the embers, do not touch
my shoulder—no more than on Sabbath nights—
I shall be dancing in the squire's great room.
O! O! come, Malkin! O Malkin, little chuck,
won't you sit mewing on the window ledge,
and grin at squire's eyes? Sick, O sick to death,
and what a brave dance shall we singing three
beat out his breath with! Come, girl.

RHODA: Yes, but I?
What will you give me if I give myself
to all this toilsomeness of being loved?

BESS: The boy for a husband or a hundred pounds:
And I and the wise devil for your friends.
Come in.

                                    [*She begins singing*

    Hey, when I saw a man in red
    then I knew that I was dead;
    he had a crownet on his head,
        and he smiled awry at me;
    smiled awry and gave me a kiss,
    and a black pinch somewhere I-wis,
        and we danced blithe and free.

        [*The second stanza is heard from within the hut*

Hey, when I saw the black man grow
and never a shadow did he throw;

  the moon shone bright, and all below
    the corpses laughed at me;
  hooves and feet went quickly then,
  and I danced an hour with two dead men,
    and we danced blithe and free.

ACT II

[A week later. Morning. DAN comes in hastily and raps fiercely at the shut door]

DAN: Hey, hey! Hey, mother! Rhoda! who's astir?
Hey there! God strike them! Mother! Rhoda! Wake!
BESS [within]: Who's there? who hunts the witch so early? [Opening] Dan?
DAN: Dan right enough! No one's been here for me?
No asking what I am or where? no dogs snuffling the door-planks?
BESS: Dogs!
DAN: Men then; no men with horses, sticks, and pistols?
BESS: Bow Street men!
Dan, are the runners out for you?
DAN: This week.
It's taken me more than that to get down here
from London by side-roads. You haven't heard?
Nor Rhoda? Rhoda hears more tales than you.
BESS: You're shaking.
DAN: I shall shake at the end of a rope
if they get hands on me. There's a dead man
up there in Houndsditch, and a live man here.
BESS: Gold or a doxy or just pretty hate?
DAN: Hate first, then gold. A good thing hate got pleased

 or I'd no profit at all from killing him—
 the gold went to get free; thief-takers' charge
 for an hour's start of the runners.
BESS: Ay; and now—
 the wood's your place, the pit by the hollow tree.
DAN: For how long, Mother? I can't muffle there
 till old squire dies and justices forget.
 No, I'm for Bristol.
BESS: There's no money here
 to help you to a passage.
DAN: No? that's strange.
 Mother, I never knew a woman yet—
 not the most spendthrift hussy, nor the worst
 overworked maid of any London lord,
 nor country harridan (not meaning you)—
 who couldn't find a sixpence at a pinch.
 Find sixpence, Mother.
BESS: Ah, the pretty boy.
 Comes wanting his old mother's stocking. Dan,
 you'd kill me for it, wouldn't you?
DAN: Why no.
 You'll give it me. Food first and then the gold.
BESS: You're like the rest. If I had any store,
 where do you think my pleasure would be gone,
 in frightening all the safe-saved farmers' grins?
 I should be one of them. I shouldn't know
 there isn't a thing in all the world I have
 except this half-roof and the curse that goes
 about the village as fire about a barn.
 When the squire threw me a shilling six months since
 I threw it back to him, for fear it broke
 the utter poverty that makes me rich.

DAN: Well, food first. If you'd come along by night
you'd need it—or is food as scant as gold?
BESS: An egg and a crust or two; kind souls that bring
presents, to keep on the windward side the witch.
[RHODA comes in from the country]
DAN: Hey, Rhoda!
RHODA: Dan!
DAN: Listen, a kiss for me,
and a penny to save my legs down Bristol way.
RHODA: Ask Mother.
DAN: I've asked Mother!
RHODA: Ask her then
what fathers pay to get their children born.
DAN: Fathers?
BESS: Slip snare! slip snare! the rabbit's in!
Weasel, you've caught him?
RHODA: Or he me.
BESS: Trash, trash!
I blow them into ruin with a breath!
O the squire's wish! O rare girl! O his boy
trammelled before the world's grin!
RHODA: Do we grin?
Suppose the village hate me more than him?
BESS: O well done, Malkin! O rare girl, well done!
Did he need squeezing?
DAN: What's this, then?
BESS: Go in;
I'll brew the herbs to-night; a torn sheet serves
to frighten them, if he should last as long.
No, Rhoda, stop. Get down to the village now—
you've been asleep, I warrant—go to Anne,
Giles' wife, and bid her come; beg her to come.

Be shy, be shamefaced, wench. Anne's a good heart,
and a power in all the farms; she pities you.
Good heart, be glad to stand by love-lost girls.
Chuck Malkin, work! O a fat meal for this.
DAN: Are you both mad?
BESS: Gold for you too, boy Dan.
RHODA [stopping as she goes]: Never this toil for him to
  spend on dice—
Mother, no gold for that.
DAN: A pretty girl!
Will have me hanged first ere she lends me gold.
RHODA: No chance of that.
DAN: Much chance of that, my lass,
  if Bow Street runners come to find me here.
RHODA: Shake your own heels then, lest they shake in
  air,
over the hills to Bristol; there's the road.
DAN: And there's the road from London, whence the dogs
  come scouring for me. If you go that way—
I'd as lief kill twice as once, being hanged but once.
RHODA: Ay, you would kill and make no profit. Pah!
Dan, you're the foolishest creature in the shire.
You never look for profit anyway,
luck-wasting spender.
DAN: Keep a tighter tongue.
You always saw and sneaked your profit out,
like a kerchief-miker, never ran a game
for no thought but the glory.
BESS: Ah, young blood!
There, there, sweet babes; we've no time now for
  this.
Get down to Anne's; and you, boy, get inside;

there's food for need—then to the wood and hide.
Hark, there's one coming—off; both ways be gone.
[RHODA goes out; DAN into the hut. After a moment or two TESSA enters]

TESSA [hesitating]: Am I—is this—
BESS [eyeing her]: I am the woman you want.
TESSA: Your name is Bess? I heard of you last night
and stopped my coach to find you. Are you she
who knows the future better than the past,
because you help to make it?
BESS: I am she
that knows the minds of those who seek her out.
TESSA: Your name has travelled half across the shire—
'wise woman', 'prophetess'—ten miles from here
they told me of you. I am going down
to join my husband on his Cornish lands,
but, since a peaceful heart is something gained
for two hours stoppage, turn in here to ask
what you can tell me of the years to come.
BESS: Your husband?
TESSA: You will know him by your art?
BESS: No need, if I know you. What do you need?
TESSA: Wise woman, there is sorrow in our lives
because our eldest son is overseas,
in some unknown land, and my lord is ill
so that the doctors fear his death ere spring.
BESS: I think your husband may outlast your son,
son being mere dream but husband less a dream,
for all the offices of husbandry,
leaving the name out.
TESSA: Well—you know me then?
I told the squire the game was weak enough.

Act II   THE WITCH

BESS: I knew the squire had bought a London dame
for some few weeks of company. You're she?
TESSA: Well guessed, wise woman. Why then do I come?
BESS: Because the squire would have a woman's eye
judge of the pretty maid his son adores?
TESSA: Why, ay.
BESS: Or that—but this I do not think—
the son hath begged you come and meet the maid.
TESSA: The son? O lud, wise woman! Gerald's eyes
when first he saw me in his mother's chair—
'Is this your friend, Sir?' 'Sir, I will not shame
my mother's name by sitting down with her.'
Mothers are like religion—made to ease
youth's necessary quarrel with the old.
So part to spite the son I came, and part
to please the father, and to please myself
the largest part: to see a witch at work
and buy such cunning tricks as she might yield
for the thanks of a few crowns, since I had thoughts
of taking up the trade myself in town.
BESS: You, my fine lady of pleasure?
TESSA: I, my witch.
O there are cunning women up in town
with monstrous rooms, black dwarfs, and crystal globes,
cost guineas, but bring guineas in as well,
practitioners of magic.
BESS: Magic—they?
What did you come to see?
TESSA: Why, you: what else?
O and your daughter if she's hereabout.
The young squire's apt to buy her, I conceive?
Do you think she'll sell?

BESS: Do you think the squire'll buy?
[RHODA comes back with ANNE]
RHODA: Mother, here's Anne.
ANNE: What's wrong with the child, Bess?
BESS [signing to Rhoda to withdraw]: Squire,
and squire's son. Anne, a thing's come all my craft
never supposed. A foolish girl—but O
Anne, was the more than folly hers or his?
Now the wise woman seeks a wiser, now,
will you throw back my boasting in my teeth?
Anne, you'll be pitiful?
ANNE: But what's the . . . Bess,
she's his?
BESS: Past all denying. O my curse
come home!
ANNE: Poor child.
BESS: Nay, but, Anne, hark you here.
I won't unsay a word of all I said
of how I loathe the village, love their thumbs
thrust out against me and the squire's black look;
hate for hate, I dare dare them. But she's young—
how could I know I feared for her at heart,
as I am all in a bitter cold fear, Anne,
unless you help her.
ANNE: Cheerly, Bess!
BESS: What cheer
for the witch's daughter, the young squire's light o' love?
ANNE: Nay, no more one than t'other. These things chance.
The squire'll help you.
BESS: Ah! take help from him!
that's a wry mouthful.
ANNE: Ah, but that's your task.

BESS: Suppose he won't?
ANNE: He will.
BESS: Suppose he won't?
ANNE: The squire's hard, but he's just. Besides the whole
  stretch of his land would think shame if he failed,
  the fault being with his son. Cheerly, good Bess.
[TESSA, who has been watching the other three, seems to see some
           one, and goes out]
BESS: The girl's too angry with herself or him
  or else too much in love to think on't yet.
  And I'm too old and hated. Anne, all's yours.
  You're a good woman. I've not thought of God
  for years, but if he's yours he must be good.
ANNE: Oh no, but we are good because he is.
  I've got to meet Giles with a message. Wait
  and I'll be back soon. We'll find things to do.
           [She nods encouragingly and hurries off
BESS: Tell any woman she's good and give her things
  to do or manage, and she's under your thumb.
  It wags; it wags. Sweet Anne, you don't brew herbs
  to keep Giles' seed from sprouting. Hey my lass,
  remember—you've begun to think of God.
  O! O! my heart! beat gently, heart, for glee!
           [The SQUIRE bursts in, TESSA after him]
SQUIRE: What the hell's this? God blast your black lies,
    witch!
  What's this mad tale you're spreading round the world?
BESS: Rhoda, go in.
SQUIRE: Rhoda a thousand fiends!
  Stand still and face me, girl, and your grey dame!
  I'll have you flogged from here to Bristol! What,
  you dare to foul me with your spittle?

D

TESSA. Harry,
be wary, or you'll make worse trouble.
[As he turns on her] Well,
go on. Let's hope that you'll be amusing too.
BESS: Has the young pig run grunting to his sire?
TESSA: Why no, wise woman; it was I that told,
hearing you weeping to the farmer's wife.
Always cheat fairly if you can. I told,
being, after all, hired by the other side.
BESS: At least, my squire, last night's joy wasn't bought
under the trees—as up in your great house.
SQUIRE: I'll have you cleared with convicts.
RHODA: Ay, that's fine.
Gerald! [She cries out the name in almost a shriek
SQUIRE: If all his babble meant but this—
If this was Plato, this was Aristotle,
and Greek, and chatter about the moon . . . My God,
girl, if you've made your profit from his talk—
RHODA: Fine profit! Gerald! Gerald!
SQUIRE: Damn you, stop!
don't dare to take his name upon your lips.
RHODA [promptly and as if wildly]: Gerald!
GERALD [without]: Hallo! Rhoda? Hallo! I'm here.
[He comes in, and goes to RHODA
Father?
TESSA: Now, black or white? Praise God, I'm grey
for neither black nor white is common-sense.
I'd like it better if they sang their parts
as they do at Covent Garden. Prompter's bell!
SQUIRE: Tessa, keep silent, damn you! Gerald, boy,
here's a mad whisper going about the lanes
hatched by this devil's brew in their own slime—

GERALD: Sir, I won't hear—
SQUIRE: that ... blast it, it's not true.
GERALD: Well, sir?
SQUIRE: This girl, of all the world!
GERALD: This girl?
Sir, when you ask advisedly ... Look up,
Rhoda; dear girl, look up. He did not speak,
you need not hear a voice again, save mine.
TESSA [to BESS]: Wise woman, you've gone silent.
BESS: Lady of love,
if you could see my Malkin! When the world's
talking so loud, we hug ourselves in peace.
SQUIRE: Look, boy, come back to the house.
GERALD: Father, you spoke
before this lady, and I answer you
before her and instead of her. What chance
brings my most duteous adoration forth
before you and your month's companion there
I shall inquire at leisure. For my heart,
I am its keeper and none other, she
alone excepted who is that heart's self.
TESSA: O lud!
SQUIRE: O Christ! [All at once]
BESS: O brave!
RHODA: O love!
GERALD: Go in, sweet. I will answer this
to him or any.
RHODA: You won't go?
GERALD: Go in,
and I will swear to see you ere I go.
No tears, princess; for I would have you weep
only for little tender loving things,

not at the grossness of the world. Go in,
be happy, since we taught each other love.
[He takes her to the hut. BESS in exquisite pleasure follows her
  Now, Sir?
SQUIRE: This is no place to talk of it ...
  Could you find no one but my enemy?—
  This witch's baby? This—but is it true?
  No, no, for God's sake no more poetry.
  I see it's true.
GERALD: All's true as she is. Sir—
SQUIRE: You'd wed her even?
GERALD: Wed her or not wed
  is but to nod a little—more or less—
  to the degeneracy of the times.
  Marriages don't make honest women.
TESSA: No,
  but honest women make the marriages
  to see those called dishonest don't get free
  with equal pleasures and much fewer pains.
GERALD: What shall I say? Sir, if you could be glad
  that I am glad, or like me to be loved
  marvellously, by one who is a girl
  only because her deity can be known
  most perfect so; if you could wish me joy—
  such joy as God had making her—
SQUIRE: Joy? Joy?
  There's a place for your sort, fellow. You're the heir,
  are you? and spend your heirship ere it comes
  on the sweepings of the devil's kitchen, blown
  about your feet in the lanes? If there is one
  thwarts me from my just rights these many months
  it is the hag her mother, and you'll spend

Act II THE WITCH

    all my farms' revenues on the daughter?
GERALD: Why,
    if that were so—you know it is not so—
    what's right in you can hardly be gross wrong
    in me who am a little more than heir.
    You are the presence of our House, but I
    am its succession and its prophecy.
    Which does the House most wrong? I keep my tongue
    from more because she is a woman still.
SQUIRE: Get away; get away; get from my sight—
    get into hiding lest I strike at you.
    I'll burn the hut down with her in it; no,
    I'll have her shipped to Tasman. O you beast—
TESSA [to GERALD]: Being a woman still, spare me the sight
    of blood—from fight or apoplexy. Go.
                [GERALD reluctantly turns and goes into the hut
    Harry, come home. You shouldn't brood so much
    nor let this longing for a plot of land
    grow hate of the plot's owner. Nothing's worth
    so much of one mind's energy as you spend—
    no, and young Gerald for the matter of that—
    and even my wise witch, if all were known,
    perhaps. Come home now; let us talk of it.
SQUIRE: Where's Carter?
TESSA: Lud, why Carter?
SQUIRE: I've a thought.
    It came before, but then I let it slip,
    and all this week it's dodged about my mind,
    but Carter's wise to turn my thoughts to acts;
    only it must be swift—before the news
    gets round the villages.

TESSA: Well, there he is, coming back from the big field. Call him here.
SQUIRE: No, but you call him. I can't call aloud till something's happened. Carter will know what.
TESSA: It's strange to call across the country fields: However—Mr. Carter!—yes, he heard— Here!—Mr. Carter! look, he's coming down.

[In a minute CARTER comes in]

CARTER: Good morning, Mrs. Marlow.—Squire, what's wrong?
SQUIRE: Tessa, go home, Don't speak. Go home, I say. I'm coming. Straight home. Don't stand gossiping with farmers' wives, and winking round the news.
TESSA [to CARTER]: Get him home quickly. Very well, Harry. [She goes out
CARTER: What's wrong?
SQUIRE: Gerald, the cursed fool, and this young brat, this squealing mandrake—there's what's wrong.
CARTER: What more? The boy's been mad on her since he came down from Oxford, and you know it.
SQUIRE: Well, he's mad now past retrieving. I've a grandson now, mayhap.

[CARTER whistles]

A grandson, Carter, a new heir.
CARTER: Gad! Damn him, he's been poaching!
SQUIRE: He's been caught.
CARTER: Umph. Well, what then?
SQUIRE: Carter, there's one way out. Two ways—for the mother and the girl. The witch— can't the farmhands try if she *is* a witch,

Act II   THE WITCH

if they were sure I'd wink at it? The pond,
thumbs tied, and . . . you know, Carter?
CARTER: Ay, I know.
But that won't hurt the girl.
SQUIRE: There's other girls
find London pleasanter than the fields—once there
she might be lost in London.
CARTER: What would you give
to have her in London willy-nilly?
SQUIRE: Much
to have her in London; more to know her safe
never to come from London—nor to leave
what cellar—or what deeper hole—she found.
CARTER: Umph. Well, for payment—
                         Leave me. You're too harsh
and if the old hag thinks to keep her house
she'll starve ere Rhoda cross the parish bounds.
Leave me. There's ways . . . and other ways . . . But
    the boy,
he won't stand still and see the lass thrown by.
SQUIRE: Damn him, if he must needs be young and gay,
hadn't London or Oxford or Bristol girls enough
that he must choose this hedge-flower? . . .
CARTER: If one night made one kind of fool of him,
mightn't another make a bigger kind?
As there's some folly in the blood that beats
so wholly natural.
SQUIRE: All his dreams mean this.
CARTER: No—this means all his dreams. I know the
    sort—
all shining fishlike scales of poetry
and shooting this way or the other through

an ocean of dark longing: there he goes,
sing hey! some colour or some food attracts
and there again he's off and deeper. Wait;
first the girl, then the old woman, last your son.
Where are they?
SQUIRE: All in there.
CARTER: I'll talk to them.
Go you to the house.
SQUIRE: That I should dread her blood
to warm themselves on the terrace in my sun!
[He goes out; and CARTER, going across, suddenly knocks and opens the door. He steps back as DAN faces him]
CARTER: Hey now, what's this? it's never Dan come back?
DAN: You're a fine agent. Didn't you hear me come?
Didn't you hear me stepping o'er the stiles?
What else are agents for? Must not the rich
have ears to listen lest a trespass shake
the midnight dew from their thick grass or fright
the wood-mice, which are valued being theirs?
Master, the rich will look askance at you
failing your duty.
CARTER: Ay, the same old Dan;
you'd rather spend breath blowing at the lords
than cool your own gruel with it. Blow your best.
What shook in London—parliament or throne?
or did you blow a coach down in the street?
Why are you back, with some streets upright still?
DAN [angrily]: What's that to you, hired spy? you slinking prig,
sneaking the crusts your masters leave the poor?
I'd rather be a kerchief-snatching grab—

let be a gentleman of the road—than you,
fattened with dripping from your master's meat.
CARTER: Most like you will be.
DAN: Ah, and wait some days:
what if another rode on the squire's horse
who would not see her brother at a loss
for want of the agent's nag? You'd leg it then
over the stiles and far enough from here.
[RHODA, followed by GERALD, has come out of the cottage. She
    catches DAN's arm and speaks in his ear]
RHODA: Oaf, will you lose all?
DAN: Never fear, he's naught.
He's in the squire's hand and the squire in yours.
RHODA: And you in his and mine—either way lost
if one word slips to the runners. Fool, be quiet,
get to the wood and crouch there.
DAN: Look you, girl . . .
Well, but I only meant to fright him . . .
RHODA: Fright!
If he once let you fright him he'd be shamed
to see himself thereafter. Know your man
as I do, and can deal with him. Yes, now,
now even, I think I hold him. Off, you fool.
                    [DAN mutters uneasily and then slips off
RHODA [calling after him]: You'll be in Bristol by tomorrow night.
God bless you, brother.
    [CARTER strolls leisurely towards her, and glowers at GERALD]
CARTER: Bristol then, you think?
RHODA: Ay, he's a fancy for a ship.
CARTER: A ship!

I'd like to see your brother twisting ropes
some hundred feet above the waves, some ten
below the thunder.
RHODA: What can my mother do?
Here's the one man that's ours.
GERALD: Sweet, forbear
to think so meanly of the world; in me,
however poorly, all mankind is yours.
CARTER: Let me make my own offer, none the less,
discharging first your father's bidding. When
your leisure serves, he waits you at the house.
I've talked and he's grown calm.
GERALD: Calm's not enough.
Calm's to persuade him in. I will not sue;
he must intreat this lady—and my wife—
to find her lodging there.
CARTER: Well, give him time,
and take her pleasure first.
GERALD [taking RHODA aside]: Sweet, if he sends—
sends me—not then your lover but his son,
his name, his second self, his house—to pray
your courtesy to be his guest, your pride
would meet his so far graciously?
RHODA: O! yet
let me consider here a little while
what may be come on me. Dear, let me rest
and wonder what a most sweet madness wrought—
GERALD: But you must swear to love the madness still
for love's great sake that moved it. O princess,
you are the keystone of a mighty arch
wherein we all are builded—a new life,
a divine promise of diviner things.

Act II   THE WITCH

RHODA: Alas, I see all things are shaken down
about me and I cannot move ... I ... I ...
Go now, I cannot think of things to say.
GERALD: You have no need to say things; you were made
merely in your simplicity to be
the meaning of all phrases. I will go,
but promise me you will stay here at peace—
peace which is all a silence, save it bear
a bird's call as the promise of our love.
RHODA: I will remember. My dear lord, farewell.
GERALD: Farewell, until I come again in peace.
[He goes out. CARTER has been watching from a little distance, and
now comes down to RHODA]
CARTER: Well, my girl?   [She says nothing]
         Well? Come, Rhoda, not a word?
Isn't this something sudden? If I dealt
in promises and dreams and poetry
and great Greek names the lad mouths out so well
I should be peevish now.
RHODA: Ralph, I am shamed.
CARTER: Why no, not shamed; I never held you wise,
being a woman—
RHODA: No, not wise; O Ralph—
why did you make me other than myself?
CARTER: I make you other?
RHODA: It was nought to you—
and I was nought—why did you threaten me
with such a loftiness that all my strain
could barely keep you from me, and my heart
strained upward? It was that which ruined me,
leaving me on my leftward side so bare
that any thief could enter.

CARTER: And one did,
it seems; but not without your will.
RHODA: My will?
Dare you reproach me, when my will was numb,
under so strong a voice that beat it down,
I could not wrestle any more? Go now,
for you have lost now what you never gained
and he has lost what he could never gain,
and I have lost—O how much more than all
maidens who lose their maidenhood too soon!
CARTER: Women will have their choice and weep for it;
a woman needs must have a man to blame,
else she is ill at ease. Come now, my lass;
all's not lost yet, but you must pick your path
through the squire's fancies. He has whims and ways,
and your young lad there—a good fellow, true,
but something cock-a-hoop to beard the squire.
Don't lean on him too much.
RHODA: I will hear all
except to hear you say a word to me
that makes him other than a dream.
CARTER: A dream?
Gad, but you'll wake to worse than toothache. Tush,
don't talk so idly . . . Not but there's a truth
in what you say; these lads are fancy's dreams
to lasses of their age.
RHODA: Do not suppose
that I shall lean or turn or look for him,
whatever comes. I know what I have lost,
and I will stand up in the void; but you,—
Ralph, have some pity and go swiftly by.
CARTER: You make too much of this.

RHODA: I cannot make
too much of nothing, which is all I have.
CARTER: Why, if you've lost your stock in trade—
RHODA: O no,
my trade is all I have. It is my joy,
it is my terror, that is wholly gone.
CARTER: Your terror?
RHODA: My sweet fear, that was my strength.
Will you not go?
CARTER: Why, what's a boy to me?
RHODA: To think I hardly knew he kissed me!
CARTER: Faith,
there isn't much in poets making love,
a shadow kissing a shadow.
RHODA: No, not much;
only a shadow frightening a strong man.
CARTER: You need strength, don't you?
RHODA: I must find my own.
CARTER: You? yes, that's likely—you to be your strength.
Come, be advised, lass—
[He takes hold of her arm]
RHODA: Ah, don't touch me! ah
I shall go mad with joy to feel you once
hold me—let go.
CARTER: Let go—for a boy's dream?
Are you a woman?
RHODA: No, I am nothing at all.
Loose me, and I shall know myself again.
CARTER: But if I will not?
RHODA: Hold me; let me die
here.
CARTER: You shall neither die nor go to him.

You are mine; you are mine; why did you wander, fool,
into a vapour?
RHODA: Ralph, I did not go—
you were not there and I was lost.
CARTER: By God,
I knew whose you must be . . . Enough. I'll see
the squire shall have his way and pay for all.
We will to London, we will—off, I say,
I must have time; the squire shall pay. . . .
ANNE [calling without]: Bess! Bess!
CARTER [hastily]: Play him a little—there's still time:
be kind to a dream, and we'll lose dreams.
[He goes out, and RHODA leans against the door of the hut in exhaustion]
ANNE [entering]: Bess—Rhoda! Child, I've come for you.
RHODA: For me?
ANNE: Aye; Giles and I would have you sleep with us
at the farm—there's room.
RHODA: Sleep with you at the farm?
ANNE: Bless her, she's mazed. Why, you need friends, and friends
may visit one another.
RHODA: Sleep with you?
ANNE: There, there. Is your mother in? I'll talk with her.
An end to all this witch's talk, and you
shall find the rest of us good fellows. Come,
I'll have my way, and we will all be friends.
RHODA: Friends?
ANNE: I'll go in. Bess!
[She goes into the hut
RHODA: Friends? Now, now to choose.
Aid me, my wit. If the squire fails, there's Ralph—

Act III   THE WITCH

squire's daughter or the agent's mistress? One
I must trust somewhere. The boy's wife—and here?
Or London? Could I rise in London? Lords
and their gay houses? Trust me to slip Ralph
if a chance offers. Yet the other's safe
once reached—but there's much reaching; there's the
   squire.
Not Anne's bed anyhow—that's too far off
and too much guarded. London? but the risk
of him grown tired. Well, other girls than I
have lived in a king's palace. Gerald? Ralph?
                     [She goes into the hut

ACT III

[Three days later. RHODA and TESSA enter from the country]

TESSA: And there's the way the world wags. Well, it's
   good.
Keep pace with it, and chat, and be polite,
but never hold it necessary. No—
never want anything with all your heart,
although you work as if you did.
RHODA: But I—
can I . . .?
TESSA: As much as any. I've known girls
come from the country and be kept at court.
You're safe; I'm not. I trust my all on you—
that's if you come.
RHODA: If I were sure the squire
wouldn't give in . . .
TESSA: O lud, and if he does—
what do you gain? You'll be a country-wife,
only with men instead of pigs to feed.

Two weeks of this have tired me—forty years
I couldn't bear, nor you, child.

RHODA: Forty years!

TESSA: That's what you're fighting for; forty slow years
of sitting near to Gerald, reckoning gowns
and telling cooks how mutton should be dressed.
But O to see the link-boys in the Mall,
the coaches going to the House, the king
nodding to you perhaps—he did to me
summers ago.

RHODA: But what's in this for you
that you should help me, keep me, teach me what
to wear, and how to move—bring me by sly
paths to the privy-garden? That means gold—
why should you spend your gold on me?

TESSA: Why, thus:
it's a fair bargain, for a twelvemonth each.
I'm aging, but I'm not neglected; well,
I do not choose to cling, and be pushed down,
step by step, the back stairs, and end at last
among the link-boys and the horse-boys. No.
Let me step from the mistress to the friend;
I know the Duke's mood—you shall be my last
victorious battle. He will love me more
for bringing you and stepping back myself
than if I pestered him with thinning arms
and wrinkling cheeks. Practise a twelvemonth—then
for a twelvemonth after you have caught his ear,
you swear to serve me, whisper as I bid,
be zealous and be true. A twelvemonth, mark:
I ask no more—you may be true for that;
I wouldn't trust you longer.

RHODA: Do you think
such things could be?
TESSA: I know such things can be.
But you must answer now: this is the end—
I leave in an hour. I'm in the way down here;
if not, I'm in my own way. I had thought
that all was lost—till I saw you; but now
one triumph more—yours, yes, but yours for me.
RHODA: Won't the Duke wonder why you left town?
TESSA: You,
you, you, my answer: you for him—and me.
Well—choose. Choose for yourself. Remember, girl,
I don't so much love living as to beg
your help to aid me. If the bargain's good,
close it and come. If not, why, take your heir,
your agent, what you will. I drop you here
like the last card of a lost game—no more.
RHODA: I close, I close and come. But do not breathe
a word to any. I will slip away—
when?
TESSA: When the coach boy's whistle calls you. Soon,
an hour or less. It waits me, and I go.
RHODA: You'll keep your word?
TESSA: Child, I must keep my word
if you're to have a chance of breaking yours.
Listen, and join me at the cross-roads.
                    [She goes out towards the house
RHODA: Done.
Good-bye, my poet and my mother's game!
Good-bye, my Ralph and mine! Luck's in the cards,
and two must lose that two may win; and you,
mother, good-bye! and the corner in the hut

E

where I must shiver that the squire may itch,
and starve that farms may fear her. I can see
my fate as well as Malkin.
           Malkin—pah!
    [DAN slips in]
What are you doing here? have you gone mad
as well as mother—to come down by day?
DAN: What I want's money. You won't keep me there
tied to the trees, and any day forget
that I need food—and I know you, my lass—
you'd sell me to get favour with the squire.
RHODA: Half-a-dozen of you, but he wouldn't buy.
Get back, if you're wise; or stay here and get caught,
all's one—Ouf!
[With a magnificent stretch she throws off all the inconvenience of her family]
DAN: To-day's rent day.
RHODA: Well, our rent
is a pint of hay-seed for the devil's chick
my mother's invisible imp she loves so well
she'd prick my blood out for his supper.
DAN: God,
you make me cold. I love warm fights—but this,
this dazes me.
RHODA: Yes, you're a coward at heart.
You fear the moon and our mother sitting lost
to all knowledge by the fire, and where she's gone
and what may come back with her, what new breath
be heard at nightfall, no face seen. I've sat
and heard the hut all shuffling with a crowd
of soft sly feet, and thickened pantings—beasts
pushing to get at mother by the fire,

and seen her giggle sideways, and then duck
curtsies to some one I could never see.
O and you roared in taverns, being brave!
DAN: If she's so clever can't she help?
RHODA: She is
so wise she never helps—except to help
harm some one, as to help me harms the squire.
I'm almost frightened still lest she should send
something to break an axle or to sit
behind the postboy and maliciously
fright him with songs of dead men's fingers twined
within his hair or something dodging him
just at the corner of his eye: not so
to bring me back, but rather turn the roads
all round the breaking coach into a maze
twisting for ever, and we never find
this hut or London or a thing but death.
DAN: My God,
can't you stop there? I don't want devil's tales
but honest things like gold. Rent day's to-day.
Where does the squire keep all his rent to-night?
and which way ride to-morrow when he goes
to take it down to Bristol?
RHODA: That's your guess—
not mine. Try asking him.
DAN: Can't you find out
from your gay lad?
RHODA: Why, Dan, you've a fresh mind.
If he come here to-night, and if I've time—
it's on his hour—I'd once grow sisterly,
for very joy of loosing. And you'd hang
quicker for that.

DAN: Ask, and let hanging chance
as it may or may not if I get the gold.
RHODA: Get to that clump of trees—halfway 'twixt here
and yonder cross-roads; if I hurry by
and drop a word, catch it as you would catch
the key of the Newgate cell you're sure to own.
DAN: If I could trust you—you can't do much harm.
Does he come here each night?
RHODA: Each night; I yawn
to music every evening, which he plays
fingering my fingers like a lute .. He's here! [DAN goes
Less than an hour, she said! O whistle, sound!
Whistle me, London; there's a stalwart wench,
London, is dying just for love of you.
Here are kisses! [CARTER comes in]
     Ralph!
CARTER: All's done.
RHODA: Done? what do you mean?
CARTER: All's ready, my lass. One thing about you girls
that come undowered, there's no waiting round
while you put finery on. To-night, to-night,
this moment ... there's a cart down by my house
takes us some miles, then on to-morrow. Come.
The squire was hard to part; his woman's gone,
else he had waited longer—but he's paid.
RHODA: His woman's gone? what, gone?
CARTER: As good as gone;
she was making for the coach; you'll see it soon
go jolting by the cross roads. [He puts his arm round her
        You and I
go round the other way.

Act III   THE WITCH

RHODA: O Ralph, so soon?
                                             [She kisses him
but even poor girls have their hair to dress;
give me a moment—let me meet you there.
CARTER: No, no; we're one now. Your hair's trim enough;
come down to me and London, and farewell
to the squire's lambkin—or he'll be here too,
frisking about the common.
RHODA: One can slip,
better than two, away from him.
CARTER: But come
before he plays his gambols. Come, my girl.
RHODA: Well, just a moment. Let me have one look
at mother and the hut—only one look!
CARTER: What, you've grown whimsical? One look then,
    speed!
RHODA: And there's one thing. You know Dan's here?
CARTER: I know.
I don't guess why. I know he's slept three nights
in the wood since you cried 'Bless him' late when he
sought ship at Bristol.
RHODA: Mother won't let him go;
but truly now he's going. I came out
to bid him farewell—truly.
CARTER: There's no time.
One look, and off!
              [BESS comes to the door of the hut and sits down there
                  Well done! now there's your look.
What more?
RHODA: Ralph, go down first. I'll come—one kiss,
She is my mother.
BESS: What, the serving-man?

Now isn't it a pity, serving-man,
you weren't born either poor or rich; there's wealth
and kingship either way, or here or there,
in soft sheets, or in none. But you run waste
between them, all you cosy middle men!
Porters and panders—that's your work.
CARTER: One look—
haven't you had it?
BESS: One look—yes, that's yours,
at the ankles, under your eyelids, when the coach
stops, and your better's lady mounts the steps,
and you make jokes in the kitchen as a sop
for the hungry beast that rends you.
CARTER Rhoda!
RHODA: Aye,
I'm coming. Only a moment. Let me alone
to nuzzle her a moment.
CARTER: Not a tick.
Will you have me carry you?
 [GERALD comes in]
RHODA: Gerald!
CARTER: That's fine;
let's have the parish up to shout good-bye.
GERALD: I am permitted, fairest? I have watched,
I think, a change of seasons, not of hours,
since we dislinked. To-night's a golden night
and makes amends. Come, we will watch the star
that brought me to you: 'Hesperus, that led
the starry host'—O Rhoda, you must learn
the supreme language. Milton will not be
Milton until I hear him from your lips.
All the great poets, I know now, lacked this,

your voice to make them what they meant to be;
even Shelley, even Shakespeare. I await the hour
when on our terrace you, with that sole voice,
the only sweeter thing than that you read,
shall sound about me as the sun's light flows
now, in a feeble prophecy of you.
Good-evening, Bess.
BESS: Good-evening, gentleness.
Gentleness or gentility or both?
GERALD: Both, if it may be. I would have them one,
and will you tell me that they cannot be?
BESS: Ah! but gentility always gets his will
out of poor gentleness. Which you will be
to Rhoda yonder makes you the other one
to that great man the squire your father.
GERALD: Bess,
believe that I am gentleness to her
and valour for her. I have talked with him;
all works for the best. He's hasty but he's good.
BESS: Good? what's good? wanting a thing not quite
enough
to make yourself uneasy for it. Bad?
bad's wanting a thing so much that all yourself
is a small price to pay; but there's a third
tribe, that is neither good nor bad, possessed
by something not themselves and beyond earth,
coming to earth through holes—and they the holes;—
that's why your father, when he runs in hell,
down the low, smoky, greasy corridors,
under the roof he knocks his skull against,
will whimper while I sit upon his neck,
scratching his shoulders with sharp claws; for I

grow daily to need nothing but my lord
the black, but he wails out for house and lands.
GERALD: Speak lightly of him; he's my father, Bess.
CARTER [to RHODA]: Now, while he's talking, slip away
with me.
RHODA [seeing a hope of distraction]:
With you? why, Gerald!
GERALD: Princess?
RHODA: Must your man
invite me into corners? where's the need
he and I should be intimate?
BESS: la la!
Porter or pander, your job's done; the gate
swung open. You're paid, porter: pander, go.
GERALD: Carter, you wanted me?
CARTER: Not you, not you.
Rhoda!
GERALD: Halt there. My father is of blood,
and may be pardoned if he speaks in rage;
his hired man has no place with queens.
BESS: O hey!
See how he jumps, the chickling; here and there
now on one's shoulder, now on t'other's. Mark
that curvet backward! there's a somersault
in mid-air over their heads. Now, my young squire,
he's pulling your hair.
CARTER: See here, I do not mean—
GERALD: My lady will excuse your going.
RHODA: Yes,
with all my heart and never heart so glad.
BESS: O yes, one other. I am gladder than you,
daughter, to see the discharged footman sprawl

at foot of the steps, for my black master and I
hate the poor fools whose thirst must needs be quenched
by heel-taps.
CARTER: God, there's but one heel-tap here.
[RHODA screams. ANNE comes in]
ANNE: Good-evening, Master Gerald. Good-evening, all.
GERALD: Good-evening, Anne.
BESS: Good-evening, gracious Anne.
[There is a moment of entire silence]
ANNE: I hope I'm not come awkwardly?
BESS [half-aside to her]: In time.
The agent there is having words with the squire,
that's the young squire. Such words. It shouldn't be;
you've a kind heart, speak to them, patch a peace:
O Anne, how nice to have God help you so.
There's few things that I better love to see
than a quarrel settled by a woman's wit.
GERALD [before ANNE can get near]: Carter, I can't have
heard you.
CARTER: Let me speak
one word apart with her.
RHODA: No, Gerald, no.
Look, I won't stop here now. Do you two find
each other's meaning. I will walk as far
as the cross-roads—and you'll be better friends.
GERALD: Do not go, Rhoda. Won't you speak with him?
RHODA: No. Let me go.
GERALD: It were foul shame, my sweet,
upon these fields to give another place,
for you are the first lady of our house—
the first and only, since my mother died.
Carter, we will withdraw.

CARTER: I'll not withdraw.
Learn manners, my fine Oxford boy. This girl
promised to come with me to London; now
I only ask her why she's changed her mind.
I don't even knock her down.
GERALD: You're merely mad.
Rhoda—to London? and with you? You're mad.
BESS: A dozen Malkins—all as spry as spry
legging it with the best into their mouths
and out again! Did you see that larger one
twitching the stick in his hand? that little mite
pinching the young squire's ear? O Anne, be quick.
Don't let them start to kill each other, Anne.
ANNE: I think you've all gone mad. Excuse me, Sir,
I came up here to have a word with Bess,
a little earlier than I use—that's why
you and I meet here—two men asked the way
up through the wood—two Bow Street men.
BESS: Boy Dan!
scramble, my lad!
CARTER: Hey, there's your brother gone,
my lady squiress. He'll hang here in chains,
fine sight from your new bedroom!
GERALD: As God lives,
you shall be silent.

[*A whistle sounds, as* DAN *rushes in.* CARTER *turns to meet him.*
RHODA *makes a movement to rush past him, but* GERALD *catches
her and holds her back*]

GERALD: Rhoda, stay: is it he they want?
RHODA: O God,
do I care? let go!
GERALD: Hold back! you'll get some hurt.

Act III THE WITCH

CARTER: What, all the family here?
She suits her brother; that's true, too. You stop,
as she stops, so she says. No, not this way.

[There is a moment of utter silence, and the whistle at a distance sounds again]

RHODA: Off, off, you fool!

[She flings GERALD away from her, and he reels between DAN and CARTER as the latter strikes at DAN with his stick. The blow hits GERALD's head and he falls. CARTER springs back, and DAN taking advantage of the movement rushes forward and disappears on the opposite side. Silence follows again, broken by a single loud hoot of delight from BESS: RHODA has hurried away]

CARTER: Gerald!
ANNE [running across]: You've hurt him. [She kneels down
 He's . . . he's stunned.
BESS: Dead, dead!
I knew it! O I saw it! O who sat,
light as a feather on the cudgel's top
weighting it himward? O squire, squire! Now buzz,
my precious Malkin, buzz him, sting him here! . . .
There's water in the hut, Anne.   [She sees CARTER's stick
               O blood, blood!
Ah hoo! ah hoo! His ghost'll hang in the hut
beside his father's twitching baby wish;
blood, blood, ah hoo!
ANNE: For God's sake, Bess!
BESS: He's dead?
Too late for peace, good woman? . . .what . . . what
 . . . O!
Delicate game! Anne, you're too late for peace,
but not for justice.

ANNE [standing up: CARTER is still busy with the body]:
      Justice?
BESS: You were here;
  Anne, it's your duty. They won't take my word,
  but when a man has killed he ought to swing.
  Didn't you hear the pretty agent swear
  that he'd have vengeance? Look what vengeance
    does!
ANNE: No, surely he didn't mean it—
BESS: Surely he did;
  ah Anne, you're too good; you don't understand
  how a man strikes. But still you heard? you heard?
  You mustn't tell a lie now, must you, Anne?
ANNE: I heard them quarrelling—but what they said
  to a word or two—
BESS: Poor Gerald! Anne, be just;
  you mustn't be too kind. Gerald must have
  justice, although he's dead. Remember, Anne,
  murdered men's ghosts haunt all those who forbid
  death for death, hate for hate, and blood for blood.
ANNE: Where's Rhoda?   [She looks round
BESS: Rhoda? somewhere round.
ANNE: Who's that?
  Bess, Bess, that's Rhoda!
BESS [staring after her]:   That's Rhoda? yes, it is.
  A coach for Rhoda, too! now if she's gone—

[The SQUIRE comes in, seeing CARTER. The two women are a little
      out of the way]

SQUIRE: Carter, he's caught!
CARTER [staring round]:   He's caught!
SQUIRE: Yes, Dan from here.

Have you caught the girl? [He sees GERALD's body
                What's that? That's Gerald.
BESS [looking round]   Squire!
SQUIRE: That's Gerald! O my God . . .!
CARTER [after a moment]   There's been a bit
  of a scuffle. I hit at Dan . . .
BESS: Are you sure of that?
CARTER: Dan slipped the Bow Street runners and nigh got
  clear off . . .
ANNE: Chut, Mr. Carter! better keep quiet!
BESS: Dear
  sweet Anne, he can't keep quiet: hell aches in him
  when he can't use his tongue. He is his tongue.
  Now I am almost happy. Speak, my squire,
  I am nigh happy; speak, and perfect it.
SQUIRE: Who did this?
                  Who did this?
                            Will none of you
  speak? Who did this?
CARTER: Well, in a way, I did . . .
  an accident . . . a . . . a . . . I'm sorry, squire.
BESS: He's sorry, squire. But I'm not sorry, squire.
  He did it.
CARTER: Jailbird's mother, hold your tongue.
ANNE: Sh! Sh! it's a bad business.
SQUIRE: You did this?
CARTER: In a way.
SQUIRE: You did this? What have I done to you
  that you should twist my life out of its case?
CARTER: I wouldn't hurt you . . . I was angry, yes,
  but not to strike him . . . not to—
SQUIRE: There's cold air

all round me; there's a bleak wind somewhere. Who
told you which way he threw his arm at night
when he was little? Did you strike him so
that he should fall so? Do you feel the wind?
It means death—Gerald's dead, and yet it blows.
You'll die; you'll hang for this.

CARTER: No, I shan't hang.
SQUIRE [looking at ANNE]: Why did he do it?
BESS: Now, Anne, justice first.
ANNE: Squire, there were quarrels—what about God knows—
but hot words and ... and ... somehow ...
BESS [intensely in ANNE'S ear]: Anne, you know.
[slowly] You know you heard him promise vengeance.
Speak.
ANNE: And ... somehow ... I heard something said ...
no, no,
he didn't mean it ... vengeance ... I don't know.
SQUIRE: Vengeance? [with a roar] Aye, vengeance. Hunt
him down! Ah! Ah!

[CARTER turns and runs
BESS: Stand still, my squire! stand still.
SQUIRE: You?
BESS: Now all's done
You're empty and I'm full. Now your boy's gone
and only little goblins walk the house
and sit with you at supper, and a Death
on the other side the table. Centuries since
did you not tell me that my son was caught?
Aye, did you add my daughter's run away?
She has, to London. Now at last I'm free.
Now there's not any creature in the world

Act III THE WITCH

to hold me in; now I am all at ease
to grin and squat with Malkin. But you're down;
let your walls run o'er all the common, Death
rides them astride and always drives them back,
till they close in and crush you. You need hands
to clasp yours, and there won't be any, squire!
Ohoo! Ohoo!
                [The SQUIRE *stares at her imbecilely and goes out*
ANNE: Bess, you should let him be.
It isn't his fault Rhoda . . .
BESS: Anne, my chuck,
if aught were his fault I should hate him less.
His fault no more than yours, and when he's dead,
and my poor wandering hate gets free again
I shouldn't wonder if it came and sat
over against your farm-door. Look for it, Anne;
you'll know it by its pointed shining snout—
you'll see it best in the dark; or since you're dull
mayhap your baby'll see it. Ask it, Anne,
ask it each evening what was hiding there
in the gutter under the wall.   [ANNE *goes out*
                   And all you else,
comfortable pleasant people through the world,
you who sit close by fires or train your flowers
in gardens, as the wind blows; you who talk
most of your neighbours' doings, all you fair
lasses and jingling-penny boys, and plump
matrons, a thing goes wandering o'er the earth
you cannot see, a thing that dark or day
are all alike to, burrowing through all walls,
that is madness, and is sickness, and is hate,
and is a marvellous thing beyond all these—

being that which first God saw when he beheld
pure evil. Into your houses and your breasts,
till you shall wither and look all awry
with twisted faces, it shall slide along;
farewell, fair lasses; farewell, gallant boys;
farewell, you comfortable folk, farewell,
but this shall be among you till you die.

TALIESSIN'S SONG OF BYZANTION

IN the gate of Saint Sophia, amid patriarchs and popes,
I saw the Emperor sitting, and the smoke of earthly hopes
went up to him as incense, and the tapers shone around
as prayers before the Emperor, sitting aureoled and crowned.

As God sits in the pictures that the monks on parchment draw,
in pavilions over Sinai, giving Israel the law,
or thrusting seas in order and firmaments in place,
and the little devils hiding from the terror of his face;

in the gate of Holy Wisdom, so I saw the Emperor sit
on a throne above the nations, and the nations came to it,
with prayer and protestation, with prostration and with vows
of secular obedience to that everlasting house.

I saw a priestess standing beside him, as of old
Saint Mary stood in Galilee, before the news was told,
and yet she stood in Nazareth beside the throne of God,
and little space to find her our lord Saint Gabriel trod.

In the gate of Saint Sophia I saw a princess stand,
clad all in golden burnished robes, on the Emperor's right hand;
with clasped and hieratic hands among the strings and swords
a princess of Byzantion looked forth above the lords.

In the City of the Caesars at the Emperor's feet I fell,
and prayed him by his providence bring Logres forth from hell,
from the years of devastation, from the famine and the toil
in cities and in cornlands become the pirates' spoil.

But high and very terrible the godlike Emperor sat,
to hear the tale of sorrow, nor his face was changed thereat
as the skies change not above us for the breaking of our hearts
when love is lost within us and the strength of love departs.

In the City of the Caesars and at Saint Sophia's gate
his logothetes came down to me, his angels bade me wait
till the patience of the Emperor should draw into a deed
and the purpose of the Emperor should answer to our need.

In the gate of Holy Wisdom as I turned to pass away
there came a protonotary in haste to bid me stay,
to bid me follow after through the doorways and the veils
that a princess of the purple might hear my songs and tales.

As Saint Gabriel to Queen Mary the entrusted message told
so I sang within the Sacred House the songs men made of old,
within the sacred chambers and before a silent face
I murmured of Hy-Brasil and the stablishing of space.

As the rare mosaics fashioned upon Saint Sophia's wall
she had stood beside the Emperor; she changed upon my call,
for I gave her of the legends, of all songs that I could give;
I prophesied before her and I bade her spirit live.

As Saint Mary learned the legends, and the bright Shekinah grew
within her and about her, illumining her through,
till the Holy Thing grew in her that did to God belong,
so a princess of the Caesars awoke amid the song.

TALIESSIN'S SONG OF BYZANTION

From equinox to equinox, from autumn through to spring,
by the wharves of the Propontis, where the heavy galleys bring
the tribute of the exarchates, unloaded for increase
of her Father Emperor's glory, the princess found her peace.

As song cries out on sanctity, as on religion rhyme,
I cried to a secluded heart in a secluded time;
as out of rhyme religion comes, from song as sanctity,
my mission ceased within her, and the princess went from me.

In the City of the Caesars, where I dwelled but to obey,
ere the Festival of Roses made the wide Augusteum gay,
there came a message, saying: 'Lo, in Saint Sophia's gate
the Emperor hath news for thee; thou shalt no longer wait.'

In the gate of Holy Wisdom, as I fell before the Throne,
amid the counts and logothetes, was softly to me shown
how Arthur rose in Logres, uniting band with band,
how man stood up to battle and a kingdom was at hand.

In the gate of Saint Sophia I was told a secret thing
to show the Emperor's servants and to bid them aid the King,
till the land should be established, and Logres' lord put on
the crown of his obedience in divine Byzantion.

From the gate of Holy Wisdom the Emperor sent me forth
down the tide of the Propontis to the dark lands of the North,

TALIESSIN'S SONG OF BYZANTION

to the ancient cliffs of Logres, to be joined with knight
   and priest,
to watch in the King's warfare and to sit at the King's
   feast.

But within the Holy Wisdom, where the popes and patriarchs were,
ere I turned to leave Byzantion I louted low to her
where her face looked forth beyond me, in her Father's
   glory dim,
as in galaxies of splendour from the wings of seraphim.

O'er the dukes and protonotaries, the exarchs and the
   counts,
o'er the keepers of the parchments and the clerks of the
   accounts,
o'er the servants of the Household, ranked in all degrees
   of worth,
a princess of Byzantion looked forth upon the earth.

For there within the Wisdom, set between the east and
   west,
as Queen Mary stands to gather all the nations into rest,
was the vision of the victory that for all creeds sufficed,
since that will was as Muhammed and that spirit was as
   Christ.

Wherefore I ride through Logres, to the times that are
   to be,
having seen the end of all things in a sudden mystery;
to be the high King's singer am I, Taliessin, gone
from the gate of Saint Sophia and from God's Byzantion.

THE CHASTE WANTON

The action takes place in an Italian ducal town of the Renascence, called Mantua for convenience. The first scene passes in the privy chamber of the Duchess, the next four upon the terrace of her palace, the last in a prison.

SCENE I.—THE DUCHESS'S PRIVY CHAMBER

THE DUCHESS. VANESSA

VANESSA: Health and fresh coronations to your Grace.
THE DUCHESS: I should not quite believe my old ones else.
 Alas, when coronations cease to come,
 what shall we do, Vanessa?
VANESSA: Live awhile
 (not without comfort) on the ancient ones.
THE DUCHESS: A dowager Duchess, hid in a manor house
 upon the park's edge, wondering if I hear
 far off the hunting horns of the palace morn
 or some recognizance of the half-silly brain
 shrilling itself in memories from within.
VANESSA: Why should your Highness fear your age so
  much?
THE DUCHESS: I do not fear it: did my father fear
 when the alliances of Italy
 added themselves against him, each to each?
 but, even as he, I keep my subtle spies
 to know when this sense, that capacity,
 fails in the taking-in of my desire,
 lets go my message, looks a little by
 to where the frosty skeletons come down
 over the Alps—ice on their bones, not flesh—
 to spoil my vineyards.
VANESSA: 'Tis curmudgeon's thanks
 for all the natural ardour of the spring
 to gaze out so for winter.
THE DUCHESS: Curmudgeonly
 let you and me awhile entreat it then
 ere the spring, like a lackeying bully, come
 vowing obsequious service, and at once

 betraying whose hand fed him to the cries,
scourges and crucifixions of desire.
VANESSA: This is no mood for festival.
THE DUCHESS: All's mood.
 I shall be gay soon.
VANESSA   Yes, when all your friends
 magnificently vestmented and jewelled
mirror their estimate of you.
THE DUCHESS: It will seem
 that I am fortunate in them.
VANESSA: Are you not?
THE DUCHESS: O yes, I tinkle and they follow, sheep
 climbing to pasture . . .
VANESSA: Scanty pasture!
THE DUCHESS: wolves
 slavering about the palisaded hut
and I the jointed meat hung up within.
VANESSA: You wrong them.
THE DUCHESS: If I wrong myself!
VANESSA: They are
 but partly serious with you; or, if all,
prevented by your station; they are wrought
by your fair altitude beyond themselves
into a mirth . . .
THE DUCHESS: Never beyond themselves—
 nor me.
VANESSA: Nay, what in truth do you know of them?
THE DUCHESS: Eyes, hands, arms, mouths, knees, feet—
 and something more
whose inhibition is in my vigilance.
I will not set a bastard on the throne.
VANESSA: If this be all, why did you choose to-night

Scene I   THE CHASTE WANTON

to hear a court of oratory on love?
THE DUCHESS: Because, though I am sad now, I shall grow
from this same gloom; because there is gaiety in
subordinate intellectual mimicry
of things we cannot still be doing; because,
because there—O Vanessa, there might be
some mastery and mystery in love!
VANESSA: You take it heavily now.
THE DUCHESS: I must do so.
It hath taken me too strongly otherwhiles.
VANESSA: Tell me then, Highness, while my woman's lips
alone to-day have kissed your hand and you,
what do you mean by love?
THE DUCHESS: Love is the change
in the weariness of womanhood, the breach
'twixt slender arms, smooth cheeks, tones too like mine,
where the spark glows, the fire of the mine, the rush
of the inviting and repelling battle
within the narrow climax of two hearts
disposed to chivalrous challenge.
VANESSA: If the mine
thrust in the citadel?
THE DUCHESS: What citadel?
The blank love was not meant to fill, I know
love does not storm; but all that makes me warm,
all most abhorrent of the blank within,
turns no more in the simple drill of time
monotonously unmeaning, but runs out
from that most infinite courtyard to the walls
blazing in action.
VANESSA: Will you never yield?
THE DUCHESS: I do not think that there is aught to yield

except an accident no accident wins.
And why, but for a pure device, I keep
virginity unconjured—it is late;
our crown, Vanessa. We are Duchess still.

                [Enter the BISHOP]

But faith, not here.
THE BISHOP: All blessing, Duchess-niece,
God send your soul even fairer than this morn.
THE DUCHESS: Where dwells my soul, good uncle?
THE BISHOP: Why, within.
How now, girl, questions?
THE DUCHESS: Duteously. Hath God
a name beside to pray him by?
THE BISHOP: You know
the scriptures—God is Love, the gentle breeze
touching the hot cheeks of the weary world.
THE DUCHESS: And what (Vanessa asked but now) is Love?
THE BISHOP: All know what Love is.
THE DUCHESS: Good uncle, pardon me—
give me a festival's license: what is Love?
THE BISHOP: A duteous carriage and a simple heart,
a ministering patience, a sedate control,
a temperate bearing and a frugal mind
caring for others more than for itself,
a gentle living by a spiritual rule,
a flying from temptation, a complete
passionless evacuation of the will.
THE DUCHESS: This is the kingdom of heaven that comes
    within!
Hear you, Vanessa?—all a quiet content,
as quiet as misery.

Scene I   THE CHASTE WANTON

THE BISHOP: Misery? Be it long
before you know what misery can be.
Youth does not feel it, niece.
THE DUCHESS: O my good lord
Chancellor-Bishop-uncle, swear not so.
THE BISHOP: This is your proper festival; your lords
attend you—your delights are all prepared,
the hunt, the argument, the dance. Your rank,
your wealth, your—everything you have and are
rebukes such ingrate and factitious grief.
How much more fortunate than many maids
are you!
THE DUCHESS: And grief rebukes me for it, grief!
I am for something; there must be a joy
meant by this longing: where is it? tell me where.
THE BISHOP: I am not so much priest but that I know
your need.
THE DUCHESS: Be quite unfrocked and tell me.
THE BISHOP: Wife—
that is your blood's aim, niece: and in good time
the Paduan embassy is upon its way—
the prince himself comes with it.
THE DUCHESS: Hold him off—
you damn me else.
THE BISHOP: Damn you? to marriage then.
THE DUCHESS: And that may be damnation worse—I rave.
Chide me, good uncle. There is nothing then
but decent order; all the beat of the blood
shall be in time subdued—there is rank and wealth,
and my poor looks for duty and pleasure: naught
to meet this sick expectancy of heart?
no satisfaction?

THE BISHOP: This is satisfaction.
THE DUCHESS: Our crown, Vanessa; we are Duchess still.
Are the lords waiting? Uncle, while we ride,
inform us of the Paduan embassy.
What afterwards may chance of this day's sports,
if it prove matter for any priest at all,
shall be for our confessor. No more now.
Sign to the lackeys; we are Duchess still.

SCENE II.—THE TERRACE

ADRIAN. VINCENZO

ADRIAN: Being greeted by the city's boundaries first
with a poor tavern's solace, take at last,
learned Vincenzo, now a second hail,
our last, best salutation.
VINCENZO: Noble friend,
you show me wonders. Never court so rich,
so gay, with such a salutary show
of colours, dresses, jewels, have I seen
since I put France behind me. Mantua glows,
not like some rough-hewn nugget of the mine,
here quartz, there gold, but all is gold at once,
in the outer as, I make no doubt, within.
ADRIAN: You come in time, sir, as I told you. This
is the feast of the Duchess' crowning, each year held
with more extreme solemnity. Each year
outdoes the rest in favour, as does she
her foregone selves outbrave, making her new
instant appearance much more than her past
with a perpetual growth.
VINCENZO: You speak her well.

Scene II   THE CHASTE WANTON

ADRIAN: O sir, I drowse. Ask any, you shall find
   how much some sloth—got while I waited you,
   I hope; not natural—hath infected speech
   it lags behind the truth.
VINCENZO: Is she as wise
   as, if you right report her, she is fair?
ADRIAN: She is in all things better than the best,
   vies with her heralds, captains, councillors
   in their own calling. O you'll not believe
   how she hath ta'en all fancies.
VINCENZO: Is there none
   hath ta'en her own?
ADRIAN: Why, there you touch us—none.
   Yet she hath tempted all.
VINCENZO: What, wanton then?
ADRIAN: Do not assault another ear than mine
   with that ascription. What I tell you now
   must be held highly—she is still apart,
   her own possession, sovereignly her own.

         [Enter DONATELLO]

DONATELLO: Messer Vincenzo, welcome. I had paid
   my duty long since, but (to speak in the mode)
   I have been in adoration, being the last
   admitted worshipper of divinity.
ADRIAN: Go to, you mock.
DONATELLO: The mode, but not the thing.
   Or if the thing, but lightly. Tell me then
   which of the several gentlemen of the court
   has never profitably spent some while
   in rides or walks or corners with her Grace.
   My turn exalts me.

ADRIAN: O 'tis such as you
who turn augustitude to fickleness.
DONATELLO: Or you that make her fickleness august.
A problem, learned alchemist! is the Duchess,
touch of whose hand or lip—
ADRIAN: Her very hand
have I, except at ceremonies, forgone.
DONATELLO: It was her fairness rather than your choice.
Her subtlety discovered you in dreams,
and left you there—nor injured your repose.
ADRIAN: Out! you have never found her! she is one
whose subtlety is virtue, and she glows,
in the tumultuous innocence of youth,
divided rapture, a St. Elmo's fire
about her masts of convoy.
VINCENZO: Is this held
her general reputation?
DONATELLO: Nay, by leave.
About the court, sir, and the courting world,
as such things must be. O sir, you shall hear
even now our best at work on't; since who doubts
but that the Duchess longs to hear at full,
under the cover of a disputation,
her fame more broadly preached than tongue would bear,
directly aimed?
ADRIAN: You wrong her; still you wrong her.
DONATELLO: I do not wrong her. I have ridden with her,
sat with her, talked with her, held hands and smiled,
as all of us have done. Is that to say—
Enough; she comes. Messer Vincenzo, wait,
and Adrian shall advance you presently.
   [The DUCHESS enters with the Court]

Scene II   THE CHASTE WANTON

THE DUCHESS: Place for the disputation. My lord Adrian,
we feared to miss you. Have you made a poem
this year to make us prouder of our crown
for art's sake than for royalty's?

                [He gives her a paper]

ADRIAN: Please your Grace!
THE DUCHESS: I will read it by my candles and the stars
to-night, new-bathed to see and hear and feel.
Alas, that oratory is less than verse!
This gentleman is with you?
ADRIAN: My dear lady,
he is my vagrancy's reason and excuse,
the learned doctor whom last night your Grace
gave me good leave to bring. He was in France
a master of philosophy in the Sorbonne
and of a large repute in alchemy;
even such, they say, as none these centuries
has rivalled, since who twice achieved the work,
in a still house experiencing the gold,
Flamel.
THE DUCHESS: He travels now?
ADRIAN: He thinks, to Rome;
in the archives of the Apostolic Palace
to study if some secret word remain
of the transmutation and the gold.
THE DUCHESS: Present him.
Messer Vincenzo, welcome. The alchemical seers
must be, we hear, of their successors proud,
naming you with them: 'tis a valuation
we take from others, since our ignorance
knows less of this than any science.

VINCENZO: Madam,
such ignorance of one study needs must mean
wisdom in many: mine is least of all,
being of the mere material elements—
precious, significant, but unfulfilled—
whereby man has his being.
THE DUCHESS: Why, in truth
we have somewhat thought on these same elements:
precious indeed, but how significant?
VINCENZO: All is significant that undergoes
process and transmutation; all that flies,
obedient or rebellious, into change,
whether in the unknowledgeable salt of earth
or the knowledgeable spirit of a man.
THE DUCHESS: Messer Vincenzo, do your studies teach
that change hath meaning?
VINCENZO: Not to the idle dust
flying in clouds from where men quarry stone,
nor to the wolf-cub fleshing his young claws,
but to the will that knows each change a depth
enlarged within it, from the abyss whereof
arise auguster giants of consciousness,
more antique genii, more original truth,
swallowing the earlier. Highness, if you doubt,
your studies miss the very root of all.
RAOUL [approaching]: So please your Grace, the orators
are set.
THE DUCHESS: See that this gentleman sit near us. On.
Gallant and learned friends and gentlemen,
this is my festival: I asked a gift,
and you, so gracious as you always are,
have tasked your thoughts here for me, as you know—

or else I have made wreck of sovereignty—
I would for you, on any day but this—
but this, for this you give me, this is mine.
I take it from you; give me of yourselves.
We have made Mantua gay, all you and I,
to see love happy. It may be this year,
as you must know 'tis rumoured, I must find
some more established, some antiquer mode,
than . . . out forsooth! I must be married. Say,
tell me, what is this love whereof we sang,
whereof comes—nay, 'tis you shall speak. I think
I am half serious—tell me, what is love?
O by the mouth that kisses, what is love? . . .
Speak first, my secretary, and speak well.
ANDRIA: O madam, how? O fairest light of joy,
how? There are lamps, there are stars, but O sweet Duchess,
there is one Mantua, one delight of Mantua—
See, I have answered myself, and you, and Love
inquiring by your mouth after his nature,
and hearing himself by those your ears to be
delight—only delight—marvelling delight.
Do you not wonder, O beauty, at the quarrel
between Love's breath and yours, when he is come
into your heart, and all so sweetly wrestles
there with yourself you pant to feel the battle?
I saw him, yes, I saw him; he ran by you
ere you descended, crying: *lo, I come,*
and even as he drew near to us he vanished
as some approaching threat will in a dream.
But 'twas no dream that then grew part of us,
it was the dewy joy of your fresh morning

evaporating into us, and trembling
through a white cloud of wonder in our souls.
This, by the mouth that kisses, this is truth—
that where is no delight there is no marvel,
and where there is no marvel is no love.
THE DUCHESS: Chance of delight then must be chance of love.
For who can bid the sun arise, the dew
evaporate, or the spirit be astonished?
As well bid youth remain as wonder come.
It may be we are children of the moment;
let us hear further; let our captain speak.
RAOUL: The duties of my office bid me guard
closer perchance Love's chamber, royal liege,
than others may, or can: perchance I stand
armed amid silks—pardon a heavy heel.
But if I needs must ask and answer, thus
I find Love—Love is but the care life has
for its own prolongation; all must live
and have no way but this, or easier so.
Life for its own security must imagine
itself desirable to other life
in marriage, friendship, or all manner of love,
but chief in marriage; for therein it finds
provision for the forms it hath and means
for the new forms it shall have. All who live—
and mostly we who live and move in war—
desire long life and happy: Life itself
desires no other, and hath found out Love
its last device, as men have found out steel
and lastly this Toledo, or found silk
and lastly yours of Delhi, for the best,
softest and surest and most spiritual sense

infinitely to save itself from sheer defeat.
Love is Life's best protection.
THE DUCHESS: O dear captain,
if Life be hated by the forms it takes,
if they despise and loathe it, can they care
to be desirable to other forms
but by illusion and forgetfulness
they, knowing, must contemn? My life shall be
insecure, doubtful, troubled, hated, loathed,
rather than fragrant with so fair a cheat.
Who will defy our captain in my quarrel?
Speak, noble Adrian.
ADRIAN: O wise duchess, a dream,
a dream, a dream is marriage, household love,
and all the intimate soft speech of friends;
covering with soft and multitudinous vapour
the sun of spiritual knowledge; yes,
earthly love is a cloud—'twas wisely said;
it is deception—that was growth in wisdom:
we needs must put it by, all closeness, all
proximity of gross experience—
by will or fortune it must be put off
under the cleaving edge of separation.
All conscious things are virginal; they grow
into a sharpness and again expand
into a clearer life, as if a sword
borne in an icy yet fructiferous air
opened in bud and blossom of living frost,
the sparkling manna that is angels' food.
Love cannot live by earth; Love is denial
of all our manners and modes of habitation.
Unless it be rejected it is naught.

THE DUCHESS: How can so bright a beauty be so harsh?
What maid shall die a maid because those eyes
study such silver infidelities?
We cannot be so faithless to ourselves
and all the girls of Mantua chime with us.
Rebuke him, Donatello.
DONATELLO: O my queen,
I am abashed to listen to you all,
for you, it seems, will needs be one with them.
What have I missed, what blackness in my blood
blinds me to this full luminous delight?
What cataract hides this other cataract
of rushing marvel? it cannot be a nerve,
a little, youthful, restless, flickering nerve,
that is this nonpareil, this phoenix, this
vigilant unicorn of the wilderness
ramping by a Red Sea of blood, beneath
a heat of malediction, this that is
complex heraldic splendour of mankind
in his devices and his coats of arms
by large pavilions arrogantly displayed!
Show me its genealogy; bring the warrant
wherein usurping Love is justified!
Alas, you have none; 'tis for ease of mind
you make it kingly; we, being all its slaves,
must not be only an ogre's serving-men,
hurrying his cannibal feast on, but will strut,
divinely blazoned, angels of romance,
consorting fabulously with fables. Who—
who can deny it? O descend, madonna,
leave, leave these boastful ravings, find your glass,
then come and sweetly rail an hour with me.

Scene II THE CHASTE WANTON

THE DUCHESS: A moving epilogue! were we masked, our
  voice
might outgibe yours; unmasked, we dare not do it,
lest truth too burningly should look on us.
Messer Vincenzo, will it please you speak?
VINCENZO: I have not, Highness, and you noble peers,
place but by bounty; bounty lets me speak,
let bounty understand what I shall say.
But have your dancing carillons of thought
no noonday peal of plenipotential rage
to challenge and proclaim Love—Love, the long
ultimate work, ultimate terror of life?
True is it his caressing flames leap out
from holes and cracks in this thick shell of earth
our spirits starve on, but O will you think
these paltry elementals are the gods
prophesied? yea, Love said Ye are as gods.
But ye are ill content to have it so,
fearing the roar of the unloosed universe,
fearing the wit, grief, irony, anguish, joy,
that serve the master violence of the world—
Love laughing to itself, Love mightily
prevailing in its work alchemical
to change our souls and sinews; yea, that art
whereof the theory and experiment
brings forth the black stone to the white and red,
with its uncouthness civilized in heaven.
We are the stone; the art, the chemists we.
And will your Highness in your moon of youth
by calculation disproportionate
be nodded into lunacy, forswear
this salutary and subterranean toil,

    which He—not you, not you—will bring about
    in your best nature, reconciling it
    to the unperturbed centre?
THE DUCHESS: O not I:
    It is for nuns, confessors, saints, not me.
VINCENZO: Do not believe it; 'tis for all or none.
    We have lost the adepts' formula—'tis no more
    vocally uttered; 'tis discoverable
    but in the operation: which you know
    in the excitements and loose transmutations
    of the first stages—ask the thrilling blood—
    but to become God, but to be God—nay,
    elsewise to think were to turn infidel,
    Islamite; to be all lucidity,
    opening from a great wave of ecstasy
    into a something beyond ecstasy,
    yea, whereof ecstasy is the smallest part,
    vision wherein beatitude indeed
    is but an accident of its being—this,
    this, Highness—
THE BISHOP: Take heed, sir; you talk rashly. To be God—
    I sniff the heretic.
VINCENZO: The faggot, say.
    O my good lord, what saith the Testament?
    I, Love, will come and make abode in him.
    What saith the Canon? This my body and blood;
    shall this be more than we who live by it?
    No gift, no benediction, but my blood.
THE DUCHESS: But to know God—and is there God to know?
VINCENZO: Ask is there aught else, Highness, but to know.
THE DUCHESS: We will talk further. But for this day's
    crown—

Scene II   THE CHASTE WANTON

Sir, you have carried us beyond ourselves;
we must not have you crowned so. We will hear.
Meanwhile—our judgement dizzies—we are young—
a girl, no doctor. My lord Bishop, say,
which of these gentlemen hath said the best?
THE BISHOP: Fairly requested, niece: yet ere I judge,
this being your gala I will do it—yet
there is somewhat to be said. I would not have you,
neither your Highness nor these gentlemen,
question too far; there are bounds inquiry breaks
but to its hurt. Degree is ever needful
in the state of mind as in the state of action,
and as that citizen who leaves employment
for speculation on the rank above him
loses himself, his use frustrated, so
the mind that rashly makes its zeal presumption
breaks its own order and endangers all.
I would not have you hold this thing for common
nor let your privy meditations muse
upon the nature of entrusted office.
'Tis more to do than be; do then, and take
contentedly decrease or increase so.
But for the cause, it seems—some doubt withstood,
some foolish words rightly interpreted—
your Highness' captain takes the crown, who drew
nearer than any to what justly is
and what canonical law allows to be.
THE DUCHESS: Be it so. We had thought—but be it so.
Captain, this bracelet our right arm has loved
and warmed and—no, 'tis rank; yet take it, sir,
but not for prize; take it not, let it fall,
'tis paltry—there, those leaves, give me! Take these,

and all our thanks—best, so. Forget the chain,
leave it for lackeys. Gentlemen, our thanks.
Break up the disputation. Messer Adrian,
call your friend hither; we would speak with him.
THE BISHOP: I would counsel you, niece, to have a careful eye
on wandering—scholars I will not call them; rogues
I should not—such as this Vincenzo here.
THE DUCHESS: Alchemy is a learned art, my lord.
Have not my cousins of France and Naples kept
professors of the science? it is said
the Holy Father hath his chemist too
or is himself one.
THE BISHOP: Tales.
THE DUCHESS: Venomous tales.
Messer Vincenzo, doth your learning mean
to rest at Mantua?
VINCENZO: It hath hardly meant
progress or rest or purpose but the day's
and the next need.
THE DUCHESS: The next need might be here—
and the convenience for it. We have jets,
crucibles, furnaces.
VINCENZO: And the First Matter?
the soil of all research, that must be changed?
THE DUCHESS: We have somewhat here that is in need of
change
if you looked deep. Do not go from me yet.
I would examine . . . do not.
VINCENZO: I will take
no journey till your Highness bid me go,
or death or something mighty intervene.

SCENE III.—THE TERRACE

VINCENZO. THE DUCHESS

THE DUCHESS: Expect you then the Philosophical Stone?
VINCENZO: Indulgently, remotely, as a poet
 muses on immortality: this toil
 of chemical search provides me with content.
 Time must be occupied and skill be used.
THE DUCHESS: 'Tis a great hope.
VINCENZO: No more than any hope—
 no more than yours.
THE DUCHESS: I had no hope till now;
 nor yet I do not so much hope as feel
 what hope is, in those worthy.
VINCENZO: Keep it, Highness,
 within the suburbs it was meant for. Hope
 is a good instrument for earthly joy
 or anything not needful; but a god
 hath prophecy, not hope, to utter him.
THE DUCHESS: May I not hope then in the prophecy?
VINCENZO: No, no; believe, seize, hold it, grow to it,
 become the universe it offers you,
 but do not hope—lest hope grow flagging faith,
 uncertain knowledge, faint and errant love.
THE DUCHESS: Do you not hope then to find out the
  Stone?
VINCENZO: My hope is in my purpose, since I work;
 but there the hope is large, the purpose less.
 In the interior labour of the soul
 the hope is nothing and the purpose all.
THE DUCHESS: Succeed, succeed! and here in Mantua!
 Ah, no—mistake me not—not for the gold,

but that I might be found the smallest part
of all the circumstance wherein you throve.
VINCENZO: I have stumbled on that trap in this last hour,
desiring to be found the circumstance
whereby you should know peace.
THE DUCHESS: Is it a fault?
VINCENZO: Assuredly; is it not a desire
that I may hold some partnership with God?
THE DUCHESS: And is that then a fault?
VINCENZO: But pardonable;
celestial laughter mocks the folly down.
THE DUCHESS: Tell me again. I need not, as they said,
continually enumerate to myself
the fortunes that, I having, others lack
to plague myself to joy?
VINCENZO: Never at all.
THE DUCHESS: I was not happy—I may say so?
VINCENZO: Yes;
and yet I also needs must bid you be.
THE DUCHESS: I did not dream I lived in pain?
VINCENZO: In pain?
The columns of your palace live in pain,
the stones beneath us are alive with pain,
all the vibrating atoms of the jewel
that lifts upon your bosom are oppressed
with the mere difficulty of being. If
we for a fraction of time could overhear
the echo of one-millionth part the groan
that issues from the world, we should be lost,
maddened, self-slayers. Do not persuade yourself
that you are anything but most miserable.

Scene III   THE CHASTE WANTON
Which being known, make profit out of it.
Be happy.
THE DUCHESS: I am happy now.
VINCENZO: Yet here—
nay, but enough! let me behold you so.
This is the image of yourself in God,
and I have never looked on Love till now.
THE DUCHESS: What am I to you?
VINCENZO: Something marvellous,
destined to sanctity.
THE DUCHESS: Nothing but that?
VINCENZO: There is nothing else that you can be or are.
Highness—ah no! your angel calls you that
when he adores you as St. Gabriel hangs
moon-smitten by the very Moon of heaven.
I must find other titles.
THE DUCHESS: None. You came
to be my angel.
VINCENZO: Dare I seem so much?
And could you need—yes, all that look was need.
THE DUCHESS: All things exist in you; you are the whole
continent and condition of their purposefulness.
And I ... can but be peaceful and give praise.
VINCENZO: You do it with each breath, but O believe
your happiness must be established.
THE DUCHESS: How
established?
VINCENZO: By no other means than toil,
attention, adoration, practice of love.
THE DUCHESS: I am something practised in the practice of
    love.
My cheek burns!

VINCENZO: So the blessed ones admit
they rested for a moment from the Way.
THE DUCHESS: A moment? all my four and twenty years?
VINCENZO: Even scarce a moment. Time begins with earth;
earth but with transmutation—therefore time.
THE DUCHESS: Was there no moment before time began
in your own past? no friendship? no young . . . love?
VINCENZO: I had a vision once—angel or saint
or maid, heroic certainly; but while
I wondered, the plague struck her and she died.
THE DUCHESS: How beautiful she must have been! You loved?
VINCENZO: Worshipped; and while I worshipped she was gone.
You were not born then.
THE DUCHESS: This is the first time
I have wondered if I would be older.
VINCENZO: Nay,
what reason, Highness?
THE DUCHESS: None; a dream. And you
—you have been faithful to her?
VINCENZO: I have found
no cause for being aught but faithful.
THE DUCHESS: None?
No heart? no hand?
VINCENZO: For adoration, yes—
though none, I think, as much as you to-day,
taking a new task, growing with new life
through your fair members—but the alchemical work
in all its exhibitions and degrees
forms me within to its own vestalhood.

Scene III   THE CHASTE WANTON

THE DUCHESS: Did you not say the labour was for all?—
and now for vestals! that is Adrian's dream.
VINCENZO: Adrian's vision. O that clear abstraction,
that cerebral delight in vestalhood,
is but a borrowed knowledge. My fair Wonder,
our true virginity is deep, and can
by but one power be mastered. Do not fear
to know it as the general do, a peak
reflected in the sea of flowing love,
the deep of sensitive delight, the full
abandonment of the body to its joy.
THE DUCHESS: Its joy? its fever.
VINCENZO: Fever ends in health,
in which delight of love the snowdrops thrive
as do the roses; frozen origins
send coolness down the rivers of the blood.
It is against a background of deep snow
the greatest fires are lit, and every lover
who by his mistress enters exaltation
beholds a virginal joy within her eyes
and in her forehead and her lucid hands.
THE DUCHESS: It is illusion.
VINCENZO: It is not illusion.
It is the marriage of great opposites
existing in the union of transcendence,
and uttering forth vocation—even as now
within your eyes there dwell Diana's doves
and, them beyond, a glowing house of red.
THE DUCHESS: What are those doves?
VINCENZO: Convoy of your true self,
you in the all but ultimate efflorescence,
soft prelude of eternity within.

THE CHASTE WANTON *Scene III*

THE DUCHESS: What is that red?
VINCENZO: Perfection.
THE DUCHESS: I—perfection?
   You do not know me.
VINCENZO: Yes—till now none knew.
   I know you in your proper shape of glory,
   such you were made—such are you and shall be:
   I see you as you are, palpable God.
THE DUCHESS: Insanity!
VINCENZO: You dare not say so.
THE DUCHESS: No—
   I dare not, if you say that it is so.
   I will be everything you say I am,
   but do not leave me, do not go from me.
VINCENZO: While you have need of me I will not go.
   But you are young—and a great voyager.
   I think you shall be sooner gone than I.
             [Enter DONATELLO]
DONATELLO: By your fair leave, Madonna. I am sent
   to say the Chancellor waits you this full hour.
THE DUCHESS: The Chancellor!—I have been in a
      Chancery
   planning a charter for a little town—
   a hamlet—somewhere in the hills—whose folk
   have dwelled in servitude these many years.
   [To VINCENZO]: Must I receive him?
VINCENZO: At your Highness' will.
   Only—your duty is your praise.
THE DUCHESS: I know.
   I will be perfect—almost perfect. Bid
   our diligent Chancellor attend us here.
                         [Exit DONATELLO

Scene III THE CHASTE WANTON

I had forgot—the embassy arrives:
the Paduan embassy—I *had* forgot.
It is concluded I and Padua
shall meet, and ... like, perhaps; I cannot tell ...
make our lands peaceful, be one dynasty.
I had indeed forgotten. Must I do it?
VINCENZO: How can I tell you? am I God to rule
the revolutions of your life?
THE DUCHESS: You have
made all my life one revolution; now
I move to a new orbit. O my master,
stand close and tell me what I needs must do.
VINCENZO: The details of your statecraft ... the demands
your station makes ... your modes of liking ... these
I cannot know, dear Highness.
THE DUCHESS: No, and yet—
My uncle comes: ask something of me—ask,
and reassure my whole capacity
by bidding it be mighty.
VINCENZO: Is there naught
now that you know you must do? pass the Prince
for something nearer—is there naught which none
can know but you that you must do for Love?
THE DUCHESS: Love ... only Love ... Your path is
vestalhood?
VINCENZO: Mine was, but how should mine—
THE DUCHESS: I know my task;
and afterwards, as I am diligent,
may Love direct me. O I can, I will.
           [The BISHOP enters]
We have kept you, uncle; you shall pardon us.
'Twas our forgetfulness, and not our fault

(Or if, most happy). Good my lord, pardon us.
You must not blame our alchemist: 'tis we
have kept both you and him from your right toil.
THE BISHOP: It was your pleasure. There were some
    papers here,
some small last-minute meditations, made
upon this crisis, some advantages,
thoughts appertaining to your proper self—
THE DUCHESS: My proper self! They shall be read.
    To-day
we will not ride; we will read the meditations—
deeply considering of our proper self.
No penance, uncle, if you pardon us.
THE BISHOP: It must be later now; your chamberlains
welcome the Prince already at the gates,
and I must meet him.
THE DUCHESS: You must meet him—true.
THE BISHOP: Where will it please your Highness to
    receive him?
THE DUCHESS: Receive him? ay, we must receive him.
    Here.
THE BISHOP: Here rather than your hall of audience?
THE DUCHESS: Here
within the fresh delight of a new day.
You must receive and introduce him to us—
be so far gracious, my dear lord. And you,
indeed my lord, leave me and let your pupil
gather herself, but O return, return
when Padua comes. Tell me again—it is?
VINCENZO: Eternally, beyond all doubt, it is.
THE DUCHESS: O excellent manumission! I will earn it.
             [VINCENZO *goes out with the* BISHOP

Scene III   THE CHASTE WANTON
I have given the first breath of my proper self
to thank him; take the second, unknown God.
I cannot pray yet, take the breath for prayer.

[Enter VANESSA]

O my Vanessa, welcome! you are come
in time to see and certify my labour.
I never shall have toiled so hard.
VANESSA: Whereat?
THE DUCHESS: How can I tell you? It is gratitude,
honour, nay adoration, nay but love—
and all these must be turned. When my heart swells
to know he is alive, he is within it,
changing, enlarging, straining, breaking it,
I turn it from him, I endure to offer
this rapture to the Invisible who made it.
VANESSA: What, would you have him woo?
THE DUCHESS: I am not asked.
No, no, not woo. I would have had him take
as simply as I could have given—to him
my body as to God my soul. But lo
he is wholly given to some huge work of joy
which praetermits me but to second him
in merely what he is. He has redeemed me,
and this is all I can do—shall I not?
VANESSA: Will you adventure this new way of love
which, if it go deep, must be liker death?
THE DUCHESS: Love, Love—say o'er the name—Love,
    Love is throbbing
in the aerial height of my new vision.
Love, Love—die on the name! this death is naught;
besides, he has commanded me to be glad.

VANESSA: Are you so fixed? what of the Paduan prince?
THE DUCHESS: The present hour be for the present work!
  Do not inquire until I have attained,
  till I can face my master with a brow
  vestal as his, and ask if he approve me.
VANESSA: And what of Donatello?
THE DUCHESS: Donatello?
VANESSA: Have you not been his friend, his peer of love,
  his Duchess of delights?
THE DUCHESS: If his young laughter
  so deigned to us, be sure he did but deign.
  He pleased his mistress, and I—did not please him.
  He is my alchemist's servant for a boon.
  Guess me the boon, Vanessa.
VANESSA: Nay.
THE DUCHESS: Vanessa.
  Look on him full and see. But first, assist me.
  I take my state; I must be Mantua
  to all except my alchemist and you.

[The BISHOP returns, with the Court, introducing the PRINCE]

THE PRINCE: Madonna, I am come, not quite unknown,
  with some applause and some disparagement
  preluding me—four victories, one defeat,
  all by great fortune and a little skill
  got in defence of Padua. Our late battles
  were neither yours nor mine; our fathers made them
  who shall for loftier merit be remembered,
  that dolefulness let die. I would myself
  present myself unto your Highness' study
  that what skill you may use to find me out
  should have such grace of opportunity

as presence more than rumour nourishes.
Our place in the world you know—our disposition
may govern France and Naples; Spain hath spies
to learn our friendship or dispute. I speak thus
for I would have you give such entertainment
the ceremonial of your thought. What more
is broached, beyond mere amity, between us
is for our servants first to meditate.
It is enough for us to see each other
as princes may do. I have said thus far
by my own will and contract with my council.
For me, I never could till now mistrust
my own place in the world, but seeing you
who I supposed were Mantua, and now find
are something other, I am made mistrustful
of the utmost that I was, am, or can be.
I do not trust myself but my occasion.
Do not forget too soon, O sovereign princess,
what I can give. I am Padua and the future.
THE DUCHESS: Sir and our royal friend, we shall consider
within our chancery and within ourself
your proffers of good fellowship: we remit
—entreating you to use our house with freedom—
the entertainment of your thought and you
to such our officers as is convenient.
Ourself as least, is last; we will consider.
                [The DUCHESS with great ceremony departs
THE PRINCE: She listened, for she answered, but her eyes
were a young constellation, carved in stone.
THE BISHOP: Take it not deeply so. She must seem careful.
She weighs the summons—
THE PRINCE: With those empty eyes?

But we will keep our embassy's promise here,
attending the full month. Indeed, she is noble.
   [They go out, leaving VINCENZO and ADRIAN]
VINCENZO: Indeed, she is noble: something other—living,
   moving, warm, natural.
ADRIAN: Hath she stepped at ease
   amid your learning?
VINCENZO: Natural, natural, still
   'tis mere necessity: I must have seen her.
   I have learnt so much to tell her but a little:
   how little is the all that I can tell
   to what she is.
ADRIAN: Messer—
VINCENZO: She is already
   become the Way; she is high up the mountain
   and I a stumbler.
ADRIAN: Have good heed you—
VINCENZO: Adrian,
   this prince is young.
ADRIAN: The meeter for the marriage,
   if marriage must be.
VINCENZO: She departed! she
   his partner, his companion! she his friend!
   but she could love: O Adrian, she could love.
           [Re-enter the BISHOP]
THE BISHOP: Messer Vincenzo, I would have you mark
   you are too near the Duchess: you are too frequent,
   too talkative with her. She is a lady
   of much concern to Mantua and to Europe
   but young and apt to be amused with playthings—
   these crucibles of yours, these transmutations.
   Keep further; know yourself, sir —'tis your faery

discourse that hath entranced her. Things of moment
are in their action—stand from them or suffer.
VINCENZO: Things of great moment are indeed in action.
An angel hath this moment startled heaven
with such news as must ever sing itself
where'er the Immaculate is conceived.
THE BISHOP: What now?
VINCENZO: Immaculacy! thrice-immaculacy!
body and mind and spirit—yet of earth.
I had not thought that earth could reach so far.
THE BISHOP: Do you mock? do you blaspheme? There
    are chains and cells—
VINCENZO: If I could mock it should be at the living.
There is one living here, and only one—
whom if I mock, it must be with such purpose
and privilege of love as make the plumes
wherewith this Maia's daughter floats o'er earth.
Do not converse upon it—it is holy.
Things of great moment—O you have said rightly,
things of much moment are in very action.
                                        [He goes out

SCENE IV.—THE TERRACE

RAOUL. ADRIAN

RAOUL: Is the Masque ended?
ADRIAN: Yes; they leave the hall.
RAOUL: Alas, my duty took me on the rounds.
Went it successfully?
ADRIAN: Divinely, say.
Such agile and such sweet accomplishment—
it seemed the night grew bountiful; we were borne
upon aerial passage; earth, sustained,

in glances, motion, voices, music, new
dimensions of experience, wove itself
into its heavenly origin, and was
at once its process and its lovelier end.
RAOUL: There is a glory upon Mantua
as if of conquest; yet no conquest.
ADRIAN: Truth;
I wake each morn expecting victory,
but not of war; to think it was of war
would cloud this clearness with a bloody mist.
O a lucidity is here! these days
our very selves are happy.
RAOUL: Hath the Prince
found out the entertainment he desires?
ADRIAN: I cannot tell: I think none knows—not he.
It may be that this air will crystallize
into some marvellous event; some new
manner and mode of loving—so much good
must find conclusion great as is itself,
utterly past our knowledge.
RAOUL: I grow fearful
when fortune is too happy. Look, your friend.
                    [He goes out, saluting VINCENZO
VINCENZO: The topmost exquisiteness of the time,
brimming with sweetness, yet no drop of't spilt
by her sunlike issuing! O the topmost flower,
the very sprig and point of hardihood!
It is impossible to look on her
without a joy, on even her signature,
sign-manual, in her hand is all herself,
flowing into expression, which to express
needs Dante swooning—less an image fails.

I die to see her writing;—but herself—
live in a new world. The day breaks in her?
No, no—the day, poor vassalage of her heel,
has naught to do with her; it is a mirror,
no more, of some dress she put off—all sun
is no more than the embroidery on a shoe
her foot neglected. O desire, desire!
O all the song of the blood! It sings—she parts,
delicate and fastidious, and I clasp
the mockery and the nothingness of the void.
ADRIAN: I never could have feared this throb in you,
who were so loftily infrequent. Pause,
invoke the absolute science that you teach;
be snow upon yourself.
VINCENZO: I would do so,
if she were not the height of cold; it is
she that I copy. Winter has no slope
but to her Himalaya. O beside,
all snow melts somewhere—if she melted, think
and I, in some cleft furrow of the hills,
entertained winter still. It cannot be,
and yet it might be; all things possible
must be provided for.
ADRIAN: Yet no provision
absorbs the polar star; that hath been fixed,
you can but note it.
VINCENZO: If her friends forsook,
nay if, without forsaking, her mere heart
needed for its expansion just my own
to do its common work in, be the chief
and proper augmentation of them all,
though they know nothing of it . . .

ADRIAN: I have seen her
as level in her nature as her foot
upon the throne's steps; but this ecstasy—
why should your learning find even her so fair?
VINCENZO: It is the deep progression of her worth.
ADRIAN: Something has chanced between you; she forsakes—
VINCENZO: Yes, she forsakes, but even when she forsakes
'tis with such genius of rare courtesies
that if my flesh could prefer wreckage, 'twould,
merely to feel her salutary will.
ADRIAN: What then destroys you?
VINCENZO: She stretched out her hand,
but the tormenting venom of the sea
hath ripped me too far from it; I am deep
in tons upon green separating tons
of ravishment and anger; I am changed
to some calamitous varlet of the depths
feeding on slime.
ADRIAN: Her action hath not changed.
VINCENZO: Her action cannot change being all ways good.
ADRIAN: They are coming from the Masque.
VINCENZO: Lest I offend
I will be gone to my own room.
ADRIAN: Succeed you
in the great work?
VINCENZO: I saw a saint succeed,
and all my furnaces are quenched with tears—

[*He goes out. The* DUCHESS *and the* PRINCE *enter, with the Court at a short distance*]

THE PRINCE: It is your Highness' favour that provokes
your servants to such merit. I have known

Scene IV THE CHASTE WANTON

  soldiers in battle fighting manfully
  grow into frenzy when my banner neared.
  My father taught a maxim that kings hold
  their place for this—that common men may toil
  the better for such stirring of their blood
  by what is unattainable and yet theirs—
  royalty.
THE DUCHESS: I have known the like occasion,
  and much observed it. We are honoured.
THE PRINCE: Madam,
  were we alone, this night should give me words
  and dare—
THE DUCHESS: A little let us keep around us
  the caution of our household. Sir, my friend,
  can you believe a maiden and a duchess,
  by office as by nature apt to lie?
THE PRINCE: If you speak, and to me, I will believe you.
THE DUCHESS: Nor nature then nor office loves delay.
  If I this hour could know what I should do
  I would convince you with my own conviction.
  But, for a cause which, if we sometime grow
  lucidly frequent with each other's souls,
  you shall partake, I cannot yet. I move
  on landward currents yet discern not land.
  Will you believe that I have battles?
THE PRINCE: Yes.
  Your face is as a captain's in the field
  at all but victory moving his squadrons.
  Or I know not campaigning.
THE DUCHESS: This is worthy
  yourself and me. I am honoured in your greatness.
  Pause, then, and if we part we shall be proud

    each of the other's thought, but if we join
I shall come to you not without a dowry
gained by—I should not say it—some small strife.
Are you content?
THE PRINCE: As long as the wide world
will wait your resolution, I will wait.
THE DUCHESS: Was it in arms you learned such grace?
THE PRINCE: No grace;
it is not grace to do as you would bid
when all yourself is bidden and moved by triumph.
THE DUCHESS: I have sought somewhat.
THE PRINCE: What, I may not see.
    The search I may.
THE DUCHESS: My servants have not seen
even so much.
THE PRINCE: I love you and I see.
THE DUCHESS: For this I could believe we were... No more.
Let us break off acquaintance for awhile.
There is a dance in the old Paduan manner
presented as a compliment. Please you, see it.
THE PRINCE: I shall obey.—Believe that I believe.
  [They part, and the PRINCE goes out with the Court. The BISHOP
     remains. As ADRIAN is going out the DUCHESS stays him]
THE DUCHESS: A moment, Adrian. Hath your most wise friend
spurned these poor revels?
ADRIAN: Madam, he retired
after the Masque suddenly to his chamber.
THE DUCHESS: Sick?
ADRIAN: He hath heard of troubles in his study
and sometimes healed, but felt not—more than I,
who shudder at them.

THE DUCHESS: It is fear, sweet friend
  (may not your friend say so?), that points you heavenward,
  fear of our earthly mazes. Rise and flourish!
  Meanwhile commend me to him. I am gone
  but to my chapel for some moments, then
  I pray him, if he choose, wait for me here.
                              [ADRIAN goes out
THE BISHOP: I have observed your converse with the
    Prince.
  May I so far intrude the needs of Mantua
  as to desire if aught came of it—
THE DUCHESS: Naught,
  except perhaps Love took some joy therein.
THE BISHOP: Love had some joy? You have permitted
    love?
THE DUCHESS: What Love permits I am at point to know;
  I hope it is not sin to say it; then,
  then to the next work! then to know my heart.
THE BISHOP: You play upon me, you conceal some trick
  of meaning in your speech.
THE DUCHESS: All things begin
  to have another meaning. I behold
  the wise, the foolish, and the young.
THE BISHOP: His youth—
  he is within a year of your own age.
THE DUCHESS: The wise, such as my master is; the foolish,
  such as I was but now and many are;
  the young, the fresh, the inexperienced young.
THE BISHOP: He has won battles, niece, and has made
    treaties:
  he has store of craft in shaping men—

THE DUCHESS: He may
  be Emperor, Pope, and Prester John together;
  he may be learned in all embassies,
  campaigns, ambitions, and diplomacies,
  but he is crystal-youth, as I grow crystal;
  we have begun to look right through each other,
  save our commerce with heaven.
THE BISHOP: Ay, he keeps
  his duties duteously. Give him some hope.
THE DUCHESS: Hope, I have heard, is naught.
THE BISHOP: A virtue, niece,
  a cardinal virtue, precious to young love.
  This talk is from your alchemist's confusion
  who stammers fuddled heresies in his tomb.
THE DUCHESS: His tomb?
THE BISHOP: What else? what knows he of our world,
  even of its courtesy? Boor and buffoon,
  but now he parted from you as in dudgeon
  at some chance word. I saw the churl.
THE DUCHESS: My lord
  Chancellor, keep this warning—we rebuke
  our lackeys when 'tis needful; but our friends
  use their best freedom. Think on this rebuke
  or take it as a freedom—which you will.
  We would be solitary: leave us.
THE BISHOP: Madam.
          [He goes: enter DONATELLO and VANESSA]
DONATELLO: The corpse-light vanishes; the dawn-star
    waits
  the worship of young lovers. O fair Duchess,
  I come to claim your waiting-maid.
THE DUCHESS: My friend!

Scene IV **THE CHASTE WANTON**

  What, hath she found a fairer friend than I?
VANESSA: Highness, you taught me where to see.
THE DUCHESS: Not I
  but this great power that needs will take all hence—
  that stripped me. I am sorry; Donatello,
  I have forgot my manners; pardon me.
  It was a sudden truth that moved in me,
  and I remembered I must be alone.
  Mock at me, as with me you mocked at love.
DONATELLO: I may mock at it still; the laughter changes,
  but still is laughter.
THE DUCHESS: Happiness to both!
  My heart to-night is heavy: pardon me,
  to-morrow I will give you heartier joy.
  Tell me—you look for joy, Vanessa?
VANESSA: Joy
  is here, and I am well content therewith.
  If we intrude, dear mistress, pardon us—
  'twas I would have your blessing.
DONATELLO: O wise Duchess,
  look from the multitude of your thoughts on us
  who do as much—and perhaps pierce as far—
  denying thought as you do seeking it.
  The choice is all; the chosen thing is naught,
  except for tribulation.
THE DUCHESS: Where that lies
  we will compare hereafter. O be happy!
  You do not fear?
VANESSA: I heard your chemist once
  say that love lies in fear not quite cast out
  but vanquished; it is vanquished in my heart—
  as when your Highness' royalty smiled on me.

THE CHASTE WANTON *Scene IV*

THE DUCHESS: A gentle courtesy, sweet, to name me so!
 Nor you, my sometime mocker at delight?
DONATELLO: I mock my thought and not delight. I bind
 my brain from any impudent liberty
 to trouble the sweet pleasure of the sense
 with inquisition.
THE DUCHESS: 'Tis my uncle speaks.
DONATELLO: O no, for what he does he does by rule
 nor found the rule but speaks it wontedly.
 But I am looking to my own content,
 her ease, our occupation, our best joy.
 Shall this fair face be scratched, her hands be torn,
 and devastated all our thickest roses,
 because we plunge among them, having heard
 a rumour blown about our garden walks
 that somewhere in those thousand blooms may grow
 the fairest bloom, dunged with our minds' manure?
 Look, the lost petals, the disheartened flowers,
 look, ourselves torn and weeping! look, the rose,
 the rumoured rose, after all search unplucked!
 Put by! put by! the things of sense are ours,
 and with a subtle and fastidious grace
 let us possess them.
THE DUCHESS: Says Vanessa so?
VANESSA: Highness, if age had grown on me ere love
 I had been patient; since love comes, let age
 remember youth more fairly for that boon.
 I take what comes. God send content therewith.
THE DUCHESS: God send you both such beauty as you will.

[ADRIAN enters with VINCENZO]

 You have stolen my purposed prayer. Go, pray for me

Scene IV   THE CHASTE WANTON

to what of godhead Love in you may wear.
                        [They go out. ADRIAN bows and goes
We were about to speak when you went from us,
so roughly, with such smothered word and gesture,
it had in any other been an insult,
and was in you—nothing, as all but Love
must be between us: that you know, but why
will you discover our honour to the world?
VINCENZO: I have entreated you for leave to part—
from you, from Mantua.
THE DUCHESS: With your whole heart have you?
Why will you not desert me without leave?
VINCENZO: My oath. I vowed once that I would not go.
THE DUCHESS: All of ourselves is in each separate moment.
I never sought to hold you by past oaths—
except that you shall break them and not I.
VINCENZO: What, dare you bid me stay by you and suffer?
THE DUCHESS: Because I suffer with you I will dare it.
Let be. I will not give you leave to go—
not by this change that I achieved to please you,
to find I had but wrought you darker scathe.
The palace windows are too bright; the song
too loud within them. Farther. Stay we here.
Why will you be so angry with me?
VINCENZO: I?
THE DUCHESS: Will you not put aside unhappiness?
VINCENZO: Duchess, can I be happy when you bid?
THE DUCHESS: I have been, at your bidding.
VINCENZO: But my heart
is the one part of yours you cannot rule.
THE DUCHESS: I will not wish it; be that part your own
and governor of all the smaller rest.

VINCENZO: You speak you know not what.
THE DUCHESS: If words would lie
  they cannot speak to you. Why do you turn?
VINCENZO: You are a Duchess, I a scholar.
THE DUCHESS: Truth.
  Yet I have been a scholar's pupil still.
  Why have you been so harsh with me to-night?
VINCENZO: Why is your forehead brighter than the moon?
THE DUCHESS: I thought it had been clouded by your
  frown.
  I cannot bear it when you frown on me.
VINCENZO: Cannot the captain of the guard, the scribe
  in the chancellery, the mere courtier, fleck
  the cloud with bright again?
THE DUCHESS: So much indeed.
  But none to ease the heart-ache.
VINCENZO: Highness, think
  you exaggerate your poor servant's worth too much.
THE DUCHESS: His worth is in his work; his work
  I know,
  by the oppression that I would not leave,
  though vagrancy were crowded with delights.
VINCENZO: Can you prefer the pain?
THE DUCHESS: What is prefer?
  I do not say I will prefer the sky,
  food, sleep; I would not rather have my pulse
  beat or my blood flow. If the burning storm
  makes all the garden stifle, do I fly
  what air there is until a clearer day?
VINCENZO: Am I but so?
THE DUCHESS: Is it so small a thing?
VINCENZO: Give me your hand. How cool, how calm it is!

Scene IV   THE CHASTE WANTON

THE DUCHESS: It is an evil prophet; the poor hand
  can by a quivering subjection tell
  when certain dancing pleasures are come near.
  'Tis a disloyal herald; sorrow, death,
  capacity entirely offered up—
  these it will never stir for.
VINCENZO: O beloved,
  why do I rob you of one sweetmeat?
THE DUCHESS: Starve,
  say rather; famish—take away my food,
  plunge me in darkness.
VINCENZO: 'Tis not so.
THE DUCHESS: 'Tis so.
  Will you deny that you have wounded me?
VINCENZO: No, by the anguish in my heart to-night!
  We cannot move but we must hurt or help.
  Not what we say, not what we do; 'tis more,
  'tis much more, holds us; there are chains to bind
  in this sublucid cell of earth such hearts
  as chance or choice hath made companions—we
  by this death on each other are impaled
  in our lives' torment, not our deeds or words,
  the central pang. This, this is execution
  done on us fully by mere being; fly
  we cannot, nor would fly: is not your breath
  mine, whosoever meets it on your lips?
  The blood that in those cheeks is vital springs
  out of my cistern. These are the thorns and nettles
  whose roots bind all our dust, which when our souls
  come maying, sting and tear their tender hands.
  What Demiurgus formed your spirit?
THE DUCHESS: You.

I

VINCENZO: Things that are truly bear no parley. You
   are, and I am, and each is more than each.
THE DUCHESS: I know, I swear, I love it: and the end?
VINCENZO: 'Tis too beyond us; fashioned in too bright
   a figure of apprehension, of too deep
   sound, that our ears and eyes may know it. Heaven
   is that intensity of knowledge poured
   through our rejoicing faculties of life.
   We are in heaven and are not of it; earth
   is bruised by the unseen tumult. Down, my form,
   to find that content that contents thy soul.
THE DUCHESS: Such a great force supports me and destroys,
   I am fragile to all outward; do not touch me—
   I should swoon at it.
VINCENZO: Ah what hast thou said?
   I am undone—bring but the touch to mind
   and all of heaven is nowhere recompense
   for that forgone deceit! Your breast, your mouth!
   I would give all this wisdom for that boon.
THE DUCHESS: If I could ever give it were not now.
   A visitation is upon my heart.
   Now, now I know myself a maid; I kept
   virginity for this, and yield it up
   wholly.
VINCENZO: Not yet, not yet. But think—
THE DUCHESS: At once.
   I am possessed with marvel; something breaks
   the seals of all my nature. Look, what lights!
VINCENZO: They are the palace windows.
THE DUCHESS: They are powers
   dazzling my gaze, guards and inheritors
   of this approach of spirit—in its depth

Scene IV THE CHASTE WANTON

  a living multiplicity of fire
  shed from it; they are singing.
VINCENZO: O mistrust
  this fanciful audition. Falsity
  hath still a thousand cracks to enter in.
  Weigh yourself wisely.
THE DUCHESS: Will you bid me stay?
VINCENZO: But for a little; reason on it; hear—
  we have much to say together ere you part.
THE DUCHESS: Will you deny me? Yet, since I may dream,
  and this intoxication may be sib
  to the infinite delusion, speak again—
  Command me: shall I yield myself or no?
VINCENZO: Ask not of me.
THE DUCHESS: Have you not brought me here?
  Shall I believe and yield myself or no?
VINCENZO: I cannot speak to you across the void.
THE DUCHESS: By all your oaths I charge you, tell me now
  have you said truly? now by all the lack,
  will your deep ingenuity of brain
  finding itself believed to its own hurt
  hold? now, it may be when if you spoke truth
  I shall forsake you ever and for ever,
  did you speak truly?
VINCENZO: Pride will answer you.
  Think you that I could bear deny myself?
  or if I feared denial would that prove
  it was not?
THE DUCHESS: Leave the event to me. I have
  a single terror lifting in my soul
  born for subordination, born for death,
  if Love is: is Love? Speak, I charge you, speak.

VINCENZO: My soul is full of terrors; if this hour
I could turn off the inflexible by a word,
blowing a nothingness thro' the sovereign place,
the universal yet secluded self
that holds the worlds, I would interpret it
to its most damage; from these moments grow
the myths of Ossa and giants ravaging heaven.
I cannot lose you; yet I cannot speak
a word to keep you; since I cannot take
the truth—it is.
THE DUCHESS: And must be?
VINCENZO: And must be...
Highness, good-night.
THE DUCHESS: There is no Highness here.
There is only your disciple and your child.

SCENE V.—THE TERRACE

THE DUCHESS. VANESSA

THE DUCHESS: I never felt the summer so like spring;
This year there is a coolness in the heat
as if the seasons, mingling with themselves,
sustained completion.
VANESSA: It was the last gallop
that breathed your Highness so; the morning threatens
thunder by noon.
THE DUCHESS: Come thunder or come fire,
I think I never knew a fairer day.
We breathe the sunlight; my imagination
sits in an altitude of happiness,
at peace with all things.
VANESSA: Will your Highness choose
this day to answer Padua?

Scene V   THE CHASTE WANTON

THE DUCHESS: He is answered.
'Tis but the vocal utterance that remains.
VANESSA: You will surrender?
THE DUCHESS: No, I have surrendered—
but not to Padua, to the sky of Padua,
Mantua, myself and all invigilate hearts,—
to you, Vanessa.
VANESSA: How to Padua then?
THE DUCHESS: I listen for his foot; I know I listen—
My breast sustains his neighbourhood as a child,
the first and newborn child of my new life,
infinitely precious, infinitely sweet,
but not the life, but not the life, Vanessa.
VANESSA: You are too subtle for my thought, dear
    Highness.
Is Padua less or more than your bright friends
or he the wise man whom you study?
THE DUCHESS: All
another kind than either; more than they,
but less and more than he.
VANESSA: The Prince!
THE DUCHESS: O God,
how marvellous, how adorable, art thou!
I am thine, I am thine, I am thy occasion, God!
            [The PRINCE enters]
Our horses woke your Highness: pardon us!
THE PRINCE: I have been searching for you a slow hour.
THE DUCHESS: How could you leave your couch so early?
    We
have hardly ridden as long. Vanessa swore
she saw you as we left the gates come forth
upon the terrace.

THE PRINCE: But you would not pause!
THE DUCHESS: I am not apt to pause; and yet indeed
my mind grew drowsy in mere sympathy.
VANESSA: Highness, by leave.   [She goes out
THE PRINCE: You mock at me for sloth,
yet you should pardon since, till you are met,
I am not certain if it yet is day.
THE DUCHESS: How tardily the poor protestation plods!
My prince, you were not there when Pentecost
thrilled in a gift of modulated tongues.
THE PRINCE: Indeed I am not used to compliment;
let me speak freely: let me say in truth
this day last year I broke the Milanese
before the morn had grown so late, and yet
I think it was not half so glad a day.
THE DUCHESS: Belike your hilt was stouter than my hand
to bear your clasp.
THE PRINCE: It is an enemy's hand
I clasp, and therefore grip it.
THE DUCHESS: Neither so
is Mantua conquered.
THE PRINCE: Padua sues.
THE DUCHESS: No siege!
Parley—stand off and tell me . . . what you will.
THE PRINCE: Is this the hour?
THE DUCHESS: I have bidden you.
THE PRINCE: O princess,
you are the impulse to achievement; naught,
done, is without you worthy. I would have
my life from you and give it you again
enlarged, trophied and gilded, greatly plumed
with honours, victories and tranquillities.

Scene V   THE CHASTE WANTON

Milan was for you; Naples, Rome, France, shall
be at your choice disposable; nay, even
I will challenge the Electors for your sake
and make their choice compulsion. I say this
because my heart is swollen so huge with love
it must act—I can do this—or it bursts;
and since I have no skill to utter praise
I can but show what I will do for you—
hear me a moment—but I know this buys
no favour: if those arms could gather me,
it would be for mere joy, mere comradeship,
mere willing of yourself to me. This morn
I bring not even Padua, I am naught
but myself now—and you are so much you!
THE DUCHESS: I am so little of myself to-day,
so wisely or unwisely confident
in the world's chances, that I have a mind
to let a little chance determine us.
THE PRINCE: You are your destiny's mistress.
THE DUCHESS: While I was
I was the child of grief, but now no grief
from outer things can kill me. If you go
I shall be sad—nay, pause—but how can I
choose which way that shall move which governs me?
THE PRINCE: I will be all the governor that you need.
THE DUCHESS: Shall you not? shall you? shall the ilex
choose?
See, if the shadow of that bough shall touch
the shadow of that pillar in its next
wind-governed motion hitherward, I am yours.
All choice is worth as much.
THE PRINCE: You mock me.

THE DUCHESS: No,
  never; least now. Your pardon. I perceive
  the soul is larger than I thought; we must
  make choice for courtesy's sake to loveward. Prince,
  this is the second time that I have chosen
  in all my life—the first was but to live—
  Mantua is yours if you love Mantua.
THE PRINCE: Sweet—
  Why have you dallied with my heart so long?
THE DUCHESS: It is the pause that makes the vehemence,
  and not the action; yet I have not paused.
  Direction is upon me—I endure it,
  choosing necessity.
THE PRINCE: Necessity
  is your best name; you are the only event
  that was imposed on me against my will
  and I have loved it.
THE DUCHESS: Ah to let the heart
  choose with its depth the thing that makes the depth—
  that is the secret. But let be! To-day
  I will be yours and happy. Let us go;
  the treaties shall be drawn for us to-night.
THE PRINCE: Why must you pause so long? Sweet, you have tarried;
  give order; let us sign by noon.
THE DUCHESS: Is all
  held in such readiness?
THE PRINCESS: Either way ready;
  my treaties and my horses—had you now
  denied me, ere this noon I had departed.
  For love's sake let us find like speed in love.
THE DUCHESS: Are you so swift? and yet I have been speedy,

Scene V   THE CHASTE WANTON

speedier, O speedier far, than you divine,
my prince; and even now I will have my race
run with its single audience watching it,
he who alone among the hosts of heaven
I see lean forth to praise or blame me. Call:
my secretary is at hand. My Padua,
dearest companion, loose my fingers—call.
THE PRINCE: Who waits? call up her Highness' secretary.
              [ANDRIA enters]
THE DUCHESS: Messer, on this same moment you shall summon
our chemist to our chamber; thither ushered,
this first—make speed to our good uncle-Bishop,
the treaties of alliance and of marriage
he holds, let them be ready: we will sign
in the Great Hall ere noon. Necessity
will have my lord of Padua and myself
joined. Go—but first summon our chemist. Go.
              [The DUCHESS goes out with the PRINCE
ANDRIA: Our chemist!—let our chemist wait! The Bishop!
This will be worth a score of chemists to him,
and with the news the messenger shall flourish;
there must be offices: in this new household
larger appointments. 'Tis upon his hour—
and in good time . . .
              [The BISHOP enters]
              All's ended. Joy, my lord!
Joy to your work! The Duchess signs the treaty.
THE BISHOP: What! is it finished?
ANDRIA: Now. She bids us lay
all documents before her ere this noon,
all drawn, all ready.

THE BISHOP: This is heaven's own work,
  and thanks thereto! Go, run, spread it abroad,
  lest she should change. Call them; they are about.
  She dare not alter if their eyes observe her.
ANDRIA [calling]: Gentlemen, hither: on her Highness'
  service.
            [The Court gather]
  Yonder her chemist lags, I have a word
  to bid him—
THE BISHOP: First the proclamation; then
  bid him do what he will or she will have him.
  Shall a stained vagrant vaunting in his dotage
  devices of ridiculous transmutation
  obscure the path of princes? let the lackeys
  observe him till themselves are called to service,
  staring lack-lustre at lack-lustre mixtures.
  My lords, there is a word, come from the Duchess,
  that you, I think, as well as I may know.
  Speak, master secretary.
ANDRIA: At your bidding.
  Her Highness hath given order, fair my lords,
  for the conclusion of the Paduan treaty
  by noon in the Great Hall—friendship, alliance,
  sealed by the contract, by the marriage-contract.
THE COURTIERS: Fair news! ... good hope! ... joy, my
  lord Chancellor!
  grace to the Duchess! ... joy to Padua!
[As they gather round the BISHOP, ANDRIA comes to VINCENZO]
ANDRIA: Sir—
  The Duchess, sir, requires you; follow to her.
VINCENZO: I—follow?

Scene V   THE CHASTE WANTON

ANDRIA: Sir, the Duchess bade—
VINCENZO: There is none.
None, none, no Duchess. It is Tartary
you speak of; there are Khans and Khanims.
ANDRIA: Sir,
I have commission—
VINCENZO: What commission? what!
you had commission; ay, she gives commission.
Men must explore the depths of hell to please
her, and see devils dancing. . . . O I must
nowise speak thus or she would have some cause
to pardon me. I will not have her pardon.
She cannot pardon if I do not sin.
Have you considered, Messer Andria,
this is the only way to work an outrage
on Love—to be so good he cannot pardon?
ANDRIA: Sir, Love . . . ? I say, sir, that the Duchess . . .
VINCENZO: True.
I spoke of Love; you of the Duchess—true!
O God preserve the losel to whose sense
those twain are one!
ANDRIA: The Prince—
VINCENZO: Depart, good sir.
I too have a commission. Sir, the Duchess
of Gama's Cape warrants me to find out
a strange pearl for her wearing on her brow,
when, in baboon skins for her coat, she squats
amid her pygmies—she the smallest pygmy:
a pearl of many wonders Love hath thrown
to daze the scrabbling and uneasy vermin.
O darkness comprehends not light, but light
laughs out to feel itself uncomprehended,

mocking the very darkness that it plagues:
there, there! did you not hear it? O sir, go.
ANDRIA: If you will disobey—
VINCENZO: She once obeyed,
and her obedience ruins me for ever.
I would be somebody in heaven, and now
I am forever nothing and in hell.
Yet she obeyed! O to obey, to follow!
To follow to her and to follow her
are one; it is to be her, which I was
ere she became the Prince and I a devil.
Go on your way; tell her you call the Duchess
that I am drunk with death and cannot come.
THE BISHOP [calling]: Go on your way; run to the
    Chancery; I
shall follow. Find the treaty; go with speed.
           [ANDRIA goes. ADRIAN comes to VINCENZO]
ADRIAN: Hold yourself firmly; he will come to triumph
over he knows not what but knows is something.
VINCENZO: Had I—had I but heard it from her mouth!
All things from her take on another sound.
I might have blessed,—fool, it was Love foresaw
I should but curse—and saved me from that pit
of cursing—that last evil—to its face.
O keep him hence! he fatly will disgorge
his blasphemy 'gainst this torment which is Love.
I choke to hear! rather the pain than he!
THE BISHOP: Now, my deep alchemist, cannot now your
    fires
burn prosperously for the bridal day?
cannot her chemist to her bridals bring
the philosophical tincture for a gift

Scene V THE CHASTE WANTON

making her plate gold as the Prince her days?—
be diligent: time shortens.
VINCENZO: O my lord,
the Red Dragon is too volatile; he flies
zenith to nadir—the unfixed mercury
looses the colour, then the seventh house
fades—all's amerced with liquid. If it stood
in the Rosicrucian fire—your lordship knows
how the black shifts: there's the first calculation
spraying the salt right: but the pallor's red.
The Red—there is no help but at the Red.
DONATELLO: Who wagers that the Duchess' cheek will rival
that red with her own crimson when she gives
her signature for herald of herself?
VINCENZO: She—O heaven must be near, hell burns so
fierce!
She gives—Excelling God, dissolve me here!
The Red, the Red—perfection at the Red!
THE BISHOP: We will not ask perfection; you and I
are old, and know the Prince, Messer Vincenzo,
wanders in a young man's delirium—right,
happy, but neither true nor perdurable.
Which passing—as it presently shall do—
and giving place to true experience
of life and duty these gay younglings lack,
I think they shall do royally—to the world,
their cities, and themselves, and therein thrive:
growing thus, by an honourable respect
each to the other, into self-respect;
holding affection as a sacred trust
not to be idly handled, as perchance
it offers now—a wanton prettiness—

but seriously and discreetly: love
being no more a mirthful ecstasy
but changed into good works and decent fame,
quiet moderation of a happy hearth,
a healthy labour, healthy slumber, void
of youth's distemper, maladies of desire—
VINCENZO: The void! the void! the utterance of the void!
Mania and gibbeting and concubinage,
all devils incorporate in our flesh leap to it.
Hell, take hell's answer!
[He leaps towards the BISHOP, who in stepping back falls and strikes his head against one of the stone seats. At the same time the DUCHESS re-enters with the PRINCE]
RAOUL: Hack him down!
ADRIAN: Seize him! hold him off!
THE DUCHESS: Arrest!
O my most perfect lord, what have I done?
THE COURTIERS: Nay, madam, you were far enough. He breathes!
Look, the head struck the marble.
                                        Lift him—so.
VINCENZO: Nothing but what was good and noble. I,
I am the worker and subject of this woe.
Nothing but what was good.
RAOUL: Have him away!
Bear him to the cell below St. Peter's tower.
THE DUCHESS: Who is on my side? If I falter now!
[All go out, except the DUCHESS, the PRINCE, ADRIAN, DONATELLO
Stands Padua now with Mantua? Donatello!
Adrian! are you mine?
DONATELLO: What will you do?
THE DUCHESS: Free him.

Scene V   THE CHASTE WANTON

DONATELLO: You will destroy yourself with him.
   Your people will not follow.
ADRIAN: Most dear Duchess,
   think upon him. This most unhappy fortune—
THE DUCHESS: I think upon him wholly. The Pope's
   envoy ...
   the Emperor ... my uncle was his friend ...
   bribes will scarce hold him ...
ADRIAN: Think upon Vincenzo.
   I think he will not take new freedom from you.
   He will embrace this chance; he will believe it
   an opening for his heart. My mind—
THE PRINCE: My lords,
   her highness asked our aid and not our minds.
   I had not thought to challenge Rome so soon,
   and, when I did, with more advantages.
   Milan may move, and Venice; for the Empire
   threatens their north ... Ambassadors shall ride,
   commanders. In three marches I will have
   my armies ready. Can your generals answer
   for their own preparations?
DONATELLO: Can you answer
   for your own people?
ADRIAN: Can you for his will?
THE DUCHESS [to the PRINCE]: Because of this moment
   I will worship you
   for ever and for ever; but let be,
   do not act yet.
THE PRINCE: We must not lose this hour.
THE DUCHESS: The hour was lost, I think, ere I was born,
   and not to be recovered. Go. I see
   a kingdom falling—do not help me; go.

SCENE VI.—THE PRISON

VINCENZO. THE DUCHESS

VINCENZO: Highness!
THE DUCHESS: My master!
 [After a pause—holding up a parchment]
 Know you what this is?
VINCENZO: The warrant for my execution?
THE DUCHESS: So.
 [Laying it down
VINCENZO: Signed?
THE DUCHESS: Not signed yet. I would discover first if our great Lord would have us central still, each unto each. I know what I must do. When all my mind had failed, when all my heart stood still, I knew. Tell me, what must I do?
VINCENZO: I also know. Is it enough to say, is it too much to pray you—do it here?
THE DUCHESS: This will be the sole thing that I shall have hereafter, this joined knowledge.
VINCENZO: Will you grudge me my leap at once, o'er all your future years, to bring me where you now are?
THE DUCHESS: Where I am did I not see first from your height?
VINCENZO: Poor height that, giving standing-place to others, lacks power of itself to move into their vision! Say, *Be removed*: exercise miracles.
THE DUCHESS: Can I remove the ground in which I grow?
VINCENZO: How can you doubt it? were you not resolved?

Scene VI THE CHASTE WANTON

THE DUCHESS: I was resolved but hoped you would deny me:
   if you will not I must deny myself.
VINCENZO: You cannot.
THE DUCHESS: Yes—are there not other ways?
VINCENZO: None, none, like this! what other ways?
THE DUCHESS: I can
   resist the paparchy and the iron bands
   of my own royal siege to set you free.
VINCENZO: That were to set my life against the express
   admirable constitution of the world,
   loose that wild colt to gallop free, then catch
   and draw it back to pasturage again.
   This only can be in the awful strife
   of some great innocence against the law.
   I am not and I cannot be of worth
   to be so reckoned. Tell me the other ways.
THE DUCHESS: I have enough are loyal to me still
   to bear you to the frontier secretly.
VINCENZO: And that were but to give me to the death
   hereafter which was heretofore; my flesh
   has festered long enough beneath the chain.
   O let me know you, spirit, as I knew—
   We end the first death; let the second come,
   mere recapitulation in this world
   of what had power beyond it. Do not pause,
   write.
THE DUCHESS: Do you bid me?
VINCENZO: I command no more.
   That this is I is a mere accident
   but no less happy; had it been your squire,
   your secretary, any gentle friend

K

of your young dalliance, there had been to weep.
We are beyond tears here.
THE DUCHESS: Never beyond.
VINCENZO: No, but you do not heed them—think of me
as little as your tears. Be duchess still
over those turbulent and insulting sobs
which shall rebel, because you are not yet
unfleshed to Godhead. O beloved, write.
THE DUCHESS: Command—yet do not—yet command
   once more,
even as the priest bids the procession go—
a ritual, not an act. Give me the sign.
We are agreed—I do not wait for you
but as my precedent and predecessor,
a courtesy, no need. Give me the sign.
VINCENZO: I lay our common will upon you: write.

   [The DUCHESS signs the warrant]

How much your writing is your hand! your hand
you! Must your servant bear the parchment hence?
may it not linger with me till I die?
Command then that your deputy shall hold
that warrant on the scaffold.
THE DUCHESS: He shall hold it.
Have I done well?
VINCENZO: Most well and sovereignly.
Dear Highness!
THE DUCHESS: Call me by that name again.
VINCENZO: We may smile now. Dear Highness, always
   Highness!
You are the fairest creature in the world
within your definition; 'tis your praise

Scene VI   THE CHASTE WANTON

  you never have, as lesser women do,
  gone outside your contained person, nor
  marred yourself with confusion. If I die,
  as sometime I begin to think I shall—
THE DUCHESS: It seems so, sometime.
VINCENZO: O immaculate,
  then, then, years hence, or next year, or to-morrow,
  keep one night for me; one night you may lie
  waking with thoughts of our companionship
  in service—after that, be wholly glad.
THE DUCHESS: I think I never shall be glad again.
VINCENZO: Think so a little—knowing you will be soon.
  Invite and recognize the approaching joy.
  We were made for happiness—do not believe
  but that we all were made for happiness.
  That grand original capacity
  must be enlarged or lessened; if the beasts
  have their fixed limits, ours are unfixed. We
  prosper—
THE DUCHESS: I shall forget, I shall forget, the whole
  of this new life and strength!
VINCENZO: Forget, but be it!
  The sundry recollections of the world
  shall pass, even in you, Highness; you shall grow
  calm to think—nay, you shall not think of it,
  more than some poet, making a great song
  of cities, centuries, and gods, remembers
  his early lyrics: shall your pomp of life,
  cease in such immaturity of song?
  You will forget it in new miracles.
THE DUCHESS: Can there be any miracle but this,
  that I was blind: you touched me, and I saw?

VINCENZO: And now you touch me also, and I see.
This is your propaganda. I am gone,
your penitent, before you into heaven.
THE DUCHESS: Do you know that I shall follow?
VINCENZO: Yes. This hour
you are made adult in sanctity. Look up;
what is between us?
THE DUCHESS: Death.
VINCENZO: What death?
THE DUCHESS: You looked
so when you taught me wonders.
VINCENZO: Ah sweet Highness!
You shall have lordlier masters ere you die,
in whom you shall find nothing to forgive.
THE DUCHESS: I never have known aught I could forgive
between us.
VINCENZO: Right; for there is no such thing
where love is as this pardon, nothing at most
but an ignorant desire to be forgiven.
Will you not please me then by pardoning me?
THE DUCHESS: I do not understand what pardon means
between us; hardly what ourselves mean now.
Only I look at something which is you
and know that ever, ever, evermore
it could as soon put out my past in me
as in my mind be aught but the main prince,
epiphany, and prescription, of the end.
Call me your pupil.
VINCENZO: Now and evermore,
albeit beatified and canonized,
and I with Brutus gnawed, nothing but that:
my sole, my truest pupil.

Scene VI   THE CHASTE WANTON

THE DUCHESS: Bid me go;
  bid me go soon.
VINCENZO: Go now. We are ourselves—
  go, lest we are not, being confused again
  with pressure of activities. All my life
  I have lived in premonition of this hour,
  which is so soft and simple when it comes.
  Now we are made each other's glory: now
  the pestilence of the world is fallen away.
  All that is now is summed in that one word—
  Now.
THE DUCHESS: Now. Before life comes again, farewell.

TALIESSIN'S SONG OF THE KING'S CROWNING

    I SAW in the new-built city
        the King rise crowned;
his marches were ended,
    his heritage found.
With magians before him,
    bishops about,
poets sang to him,
    peasants cried out.
Logres lay round him,
    city-entwined,
the King in his kingdom,
    man in his mind.

I asked in a field of peasants
    Whence comes the King?
Short time from sowing
    spared they to sing.
One looked up, saying:
    *All in our dearth
Arthur came to us
    as corn from earth.
He that plucks good wheat
    knows not how it grew,
so came King Arthur
    our famine through.*

I asked in a hall of bishops
    Whence comes he?
Silent they gazed at
    Wise Canterbury:
Lo now, where Isaac's son
    (said he) *once slept*

TALIESSIN'S SONG OF THE KING'S CROWNING

down a great stairway
  Arthur hath stept.
In vision I saw him
  set foot on our ground,
even crowned as the least soul
  God made is crowned.

I asked in a garden of poets
  Whence comes the King?
Legend and fable
  leapt they to sing.
Ah son of Brutus!
  ah child of Troy!
Look how antiquity
  breaks in new joy!
Yet one from southward
  led all the choir,
singing a child that came
  in a sea of fire.

I asked in a chamber of wizards
  Whence comes he?
Sooth was their answer
  or glamoury?
Marvellous ancestors
  in a deep glass
through an aeon of aeons
  caused they to pass:
fish and amphibia,
  serpent and ape—
Human heart, human thought,
  and human shape.

TALIESSIN'S SONG OF THE KING'S CROWNING

    I asked in a hall of heralds:
       What coat hath he borne?
    They showed it: lo, azure,
       a unicorn
    courant proper—ah so
       through a jungle he came!—
    maned and unguled or,
       and gorged of the same
    royally; a dragon
       couchant gules for crest;
    the motto: Et homo rex
       factus est.

THE RITE OF THE PASSION

After some opening ceremony,[1] *the persons of the presentation enter in procession—a* HERALD *first, followed by five* MINSTRELS; *then, side by side,* JAMES *and* PILATE, PETER *and* CAIAPHAS, JOHN *and* HEROD, MARY *and* JUDAS; *after them, between* GABRIEL *and* SATAN, LOVE *vestmented in a crimson cope or other convenient apparel. The* MINSTRELS *take their places below the platform; the* HERALD *upon it at the front corner. The other persons are distributed about it,* LOVE'S *friends to his right, and his enemies to his left, he himself being at the back, with* GABRIEL *and* SATAN *on either hand. Each moves forward as he first speaks; thereafter they dispose themselves as may be agreed.*

[1] The hymns sung are given on p. 191.

PART I

THE HERALD

Ho all you people, who are come
out of your huts through Christendom
in vigil here to bear a part,
being obedient to that art
whereby a new thing shall be made
and presently in you displayed
when nothing is that is not He,
enter into this mystery.

Ye who already out of dearth
find Him renewed within your earth,
who practised everywhere and long
submission to that only Strong,
growing more sure thereof by all
good or ill chance that did befall—
your end is found, your heart is He,
enter into this mystery.

Ye who go seeking Him and find
at whiles His breath within your mind,
but more of sighs and bloody tears,
nor any rescue through the years,
think that ye, being thus sacrificed,
image and are the death of Christ;
Despair ye? your despair is He;
enter into this mystery.

Ye to whom all His world is dark
save where He glows, a ruddy spark,
a natural portent, sent to show
who will not know Him still shall know;

He, thrust from peace, determines war,
and being not friend is conqueror—
yea, fear; yea, fly; exile is He—
enter into this mystery.

Behold, O people, as may fit
your reach and spiritual wit,
the tale of Golgotha the mount—
either that which gospellers recount,
or that which ye have found within
when in yourselves He is made sin:
Lift up your hearts: all this is He:
enter into this mystery.

Hear now the lords of heaven and hell—
God's swiftest runner, Gabriel,
the nuncio to the maid; and that
Satan, whom all ye marvel at:
not knowing him through your innermost,
dark viceroy of the Holy Ghost:
Lift up your hearts; these both are He—
enter into this mystery.

GABRIEL

I, Gabriel, stand up between earth and heaven;
   I am the troth in all hours tender and gay,
the giving of all things when all things are given;
   I am the right-hand pillar of the way.

SATAN

I, Satan, stand up between earth and heaven,
   I am contradiction and entire dismay;
the sharp divorce when all things are not given;
   I am the left-hand pillar of the way.

GABRIEL

I am the moment of presence and of vision,
   the undivined beheld, the unseen displayed,
o'ermounting the after anguish and derision;
   I am the salutation to the maid.

SATAN

I am the exile following in sorrow
   making man of that moment still afraid;
I am the mockery of the long to-morrow;
   I am the seven swords piercing thro' the maid.

GABRIEL

I am the light that comes in speed and wonder,
   the light that shines though the dark is not done,
dissolving the thick chains of hell asunder;
   I am the first gleam of the arisen Sun.

SATAN

I am the thick maze and the fond inventions
   whereby men hurry from repose to war,
I am the all but infinite dissensions,
   I am chaos and the love man hath therefor.

LOVE

But I am still the end and reconciling;
   I am all things driven on through hell to heaven;
I am the purifying and defiling,
   I am the union, perfected or riven.
There is none on earth that can have place beside me,
   nor any of all the angels that is God;
there is none can know what mysteries betide me
   who am those mysteries and their period.

Long since my first Nativity have ye studied
   when the Unsleeping Word at length found sleep,
and, after, went with head and side unbloodied,
   sowing the love that all his folk shall reap.

Remember the sweetness of that first salvation;
   yea, ere ye now to paths of Golgotha move,
renew, O people, the first adoration
   when your hearts fainted at the birth of Love.

One of the MINSTRELS

Three kings rode in to Bethlehem
   from Zion hastily:
when Joseph opened door to them
   they entered in all three.

The Child upon Our Lady's lap
   the kings bowed down before:
to see this wonder, by good hap,
   the slaves thronged at the door.

The first king fell upon his face:
   'O Child, a sign behold;
the princes of the Gentile race
   offer a gift of gold.'
Our Lady shuddered in her place:
   for riches men are sold.

'I wot that when thou goest up
   unto thy throne of might,
'tis I shall bear the golden cup,
   and come into thy sight.'

THE RITE OF THE PASSION

Humbly the second king kneeled down.
  'O Child, thy dignity
behold, in frankincense foreshown,
  take thou this gift from me.'
Our Lady covered with her gown
  her eyes from perjury.

'I wot that when with offering
  thou seest thy Father's face,
'Tis I that shall the censer swing
  in that most holy place.'

The third stood forth and bowed his head.
  'I bring a gift of myrrh.'
Our Lady crossed herself for dread
  when he looked down on her.
'I bring a gift, O Child,' he said,
  'meet for thy sepulchre.

'I wot that when thy lips are dumb
  and men defile thy head,
'tis I shall wait thee till thou come
  to be among the dead.

'When thou art neither king nor priest,
  thou shalt be friend to me,
when thou of all slain men art least,
  'tis I shall neighbour thee.

'But when thou sway'st thy golden rod
  or drinkest the new wine,
or goest in before thy God,
  with minstrelsy divine,

     "tis I of whom within thy breast
        the hidden pledge shall be,
     the prayer wherewith thou art possessed
        shall be a prayer for me.'

  The Child upon Our Lady's lap
     the kings bowed down before:
  to see this wonder, by good hap,
     the slaves thronged at the door.

  Three kings rode out from Bethelehem
     to eastward hastily.
  Our Lady caught, to save from them,
     the Child upon her knee.

LOVE

Then was the time when I on pilgrimage
   must go, and pass the whole round world about:
behold, your hearts were taken for my stage,
   and thereon now I call my chosen out:

twelve masters, twelve foundation stones of man
   at his creation builded into place,
twelve apostolic chieftains of his clan
   judging his world, twelve principles of grace:

of whom to-day I show you but these four—
   Peter who testifies how once I shone,
James who still feeds the fatherless and poor,
   And young Desire of Love, whose name is John:

Also Desire who hungers for quick gain,
   the necessary grudge that in you dwells
against my patience, your chief thorn of pain,
   Judas, the gate that opens on the hells.

Part I   THE RITE OF THE PASSION

For think not but hell hath its part in all
   that follow me, at my high feast to sit;
hear the world's captains utter now their call,
   ere each be yet changed to his opposite.

PETER

I, Peter, hastened to follow: in great awe
I also thy Transfiguration saw,
it was I who cried to thee: *Thou art the Lord*,
and I who struck to save thee with the sword.

JAMES

I, James, came forth to follow; yea, being called,
I, Boanerges, by thy might was thralled:
who would have smitten a thankless town with fire,
but find my anger changed to thy desire.

JOHN

I, John, have seen thee and have darkly known,
being also called and numbered with thine own;
with a voice of thunder have I cried for thee,
but O what dove's wings enter now in me!

LOVE

Yet have I one is mightier than all these,
who are her children and capacities;
they are friends and followers and apostles—she
is the soul that is chosen to be the mother of me.

MARY

O Son, long since in Cana at thy feast
did I not turn to thee when the wine had ceased?
but now I look on the whole world and see
there is no wine anywhere nor any glee,

but an end to feasting and an end to mirth
and cruel habitations through the earth,
and the mind unhappy and the soul undone;
therefore now I cry again to thee, O Son,
for entreaty, for a summons and a sign,
O Love, O blessed Love, they have no wine!

LOVE

Shall I not answer as then I answered thee—
O lady, what is that to thee and me?
We being perfected in our delight,
thou found in me and I in thee aright,
O elect soul, must we our joy unbind
to seek the dread salvation of mankind?
O miracle of grace, consider still,
know'st thou what doom this summons must fulfil?

MARY

They have no wine.

LOVE

   Wilt thou have me pour out
that wine which is I to ease them in their drought?
All that is mine, O mother, is also thine:
what wilt thou have me do?

MARY

       They have no wine. (2)

PART II

THE HERALD

We have seen Love in his years of ministry; yea,
we have seen him walking upon the world's highway,
   publicly vassal to folk of every sort,
a scavenger and a scribe, a prince and a priest,
nor ever his care hath stayed or his labour ceased;
   but who hath believed our report?

In twilit lanes his godhead of glory went
veiling his youthful lovers, or where the consent
   of friendship made peace more peaceful, at Caesar's court
where the high fair lords his gracious epiphany knew,
he at once, he only, and all things obeyed thereto:
   but who hath believed our report?

In miracles often, in parables often, he reigned
serving, and nowise the lowest task disdained,
   but the moment was secret, the moment was all too short;
and who shall remember? who shall be wise to know
that the light shall pass but the presence shall never go?
   who hath believed our report?

Who? unto whom is the arm of the Lord revealed?
who, being once by the glory amazed and healed,
   believes a myth that the tales of the world distort?
He is despised and rejected: and whose face is hid?
He is afflicted: who hath not mocked him and chid?
   who hath believed our report?

Who will cry to him *Love!* who will cry to him *Love, our
    fair lord?*
now when he gives no beauty and no reward,
    when the hounds are on him, the horns are blowing
        the mort,
when the young god's face is pallid with stress of pain,
and he cries on his godhead, and nothing makes answer
        again—
    who hath believed our report?

Wonderful—lo, his wonder is blown away;
Counsellor—who shall ask counsel of him to-day?
    The Everlasting Father—his time is short;
the Mighty God—and his strength is less than a breath;
the Prince of Peace—but peace is come to its death;
    who hath believed our report?

Who will confess him now when the great sun dies?
who will confess him now in a darkness of sighs?
    who will confess him—after a foolish sort,
saying: *Thine only, thine, will I choose to be*—
who will confess him? who will betray him and flee?
    who hath believed our report?

LOVE

Lo I who once did your young beauty bless
now go upon my Father's business
into your clamorous market-place of sin.

PETER

Lord, thou art come now to its entering-in;
hear'st thou not how it shouts to welcome thee?

LOVE

All lovers have desired to look on me:
whose very nerves and sinews shake when I,
riding upon an ass, do first draw nigh.

JOHN

Lord, in thy kingdom seat us at thy side!

LOVE

Yea, can ye undergo what shall betide?

JOHN

Thy cup and thy baptism!

LOVE

    No reward
give I though ye shall call me friend and lord.
I am the sole-begotten of Destiny,
and am your friend,—

JOHN

    Only, O lord Love, be
still with us!

LOVE

  Even now to the priests and scribes,
the rich men and the fierce barbarian tribes,
am I betrayed! and, led through my own band,
the feet of those who buy me are at hand!

JOHN

Lord, who is he hath sold thee to their wish?

LOVE
Behold, his hand with yours is in the dish
of daily food, his blood with yours hath run,
and what your weakness thought, his strength hath done.
Ye shall not move to save what he shall break,
he shall betray and all you shall forsake.

PETER
Though all forsake thee I will never fly!

LOVE
Before the cock crow on the day I die,
thou, my strong stone, shalt also fall on me
and I be broken, but even then on thee
will I too fall and splinter utterly
into fine powder, till the day shall come
when I shall build thee up to Christendom.

SATAN [to JUDAS]
Chosen of all Love's fellowship to sit
at the receipt of custom, being fit
to rule the exchanges of the flesh with God,
of the companions who with Love have trod
art thou the world's twelfth, keeper of the purse
and precious golden good Love doth disburse
with spendthrift zeal to gain some far delight
long promised thee but never brought to sight,—
good which this present moment might have graced:
O Judas, to what purpose is this waste?

JUDAS
Meseems a great necessity is near,
and many virtues whisper in my ear.

Part II   THE RITE OF THE PASSION

Intelligence bids break an outworn vow,
Desire saith 'Buy', and Prudence saith 'Buy now,
with Love's own person buy this present good'.
And ere these others too have understood,
to the world will I hasten, even I,
silver to gain, while they their foe shall buy,
such a great wealth is wholly mine to spend.

LOVE [to JUDAS]

That which thou hast to do, do quickly, friend!
Ere I shall wound thy head wound thou my heel.
[To the others]
But ye, who never sat at any meal
but as a Passover and memory
of your long exodus from the world to me,
I gather myself, I give myself, I grow
into the harvest of the seed ye sow:
I will be bread, and more than bread; and wine
and more than wine. I cry, *Come, come and dine
on Me in yours: be new-emparadised,
take in your daily food your daily Christ.*

SATAN

Also these have I overcome, not he,
Judas, alone, but even those great three
who were Love's chiefest heads of testimony:
Herod, who is Desire turned all to lust
of wealth, mad, miserable, and unjust,—
How art thou fallen, O John, O thou Desire!—
And Caiaphas the priest whom Sinai's fire
consumes no more, but Custom, that great cry,
barks in his voice at all steps equally.—

How art thou fallen, O Peter, O strong word!—
And Pilate, who is Service no more stirred
with passion, chill and weary government
by kings grown hopelessly benevolent.—
How art thou fallen, O James, when Love is naught!
These princes of destruction have I taught
to make Love void for ever, till his head
by time and earth and death is coverèd,
Love's servants to Love's self proving untrue.

JUDAS
What shall I have if I yield him unto you?

HEROD
Ten silver pieces,—and thy lusts withal.

CAIAPHAS
Ten,—and deaf ears for any new love's call.

PILATE
Ten,—and a rest from the journey that wearieth.

JUDAS
Follow.

LOVE
Ah, ah, I am weary unto death.
Tarry ye here while I shall go and pray;
O if this hour, my God, might pass away!

JOHN
Judas is gone, and in our souls' dark night
slumber hath seized upon me; fails my sight.

HEROD
Out of the lustful heart hath come forth might.

Part II   THE RITE OF THE PASSION

PETER
The word is lost he gave his folk to keep,
and we his church are fallen upon sleep.

CAIAPHAS
The gates are down; close and more close we creep.

JAMES
With eyes by utter weariness defiled
drowsily goes my care for wife and child.

PILATE
Now fades the dream whereby man was beguiled.

MARY
O Peter, keep good watch!—He sleeps. O John!
O James!—They sleep, and hark what feet come on!
O you his servants! wake; wake! Ah, 'tis you
in evil shapes, with blackening hearts, rush through—
the sword, the sword, the last sword pierces me!

LOVE
O lady, what is that to thee and me?

JUDAS
Whomever I shall kiss, that same is he.

LOVE
Could ye not watch? Friend, wherefore art thou come?

SATAN
Friend, he is mine and thine, the very sum
of all the world's betrayal: in this hour
God upon God hath loosed all Godhead's power.

One of the MINSTRELS

Three are the thrones that stand
   in the mid place of the world,
the trumpets by them sound
   and the banners are unfurled.
Three masters judge mankind
   where the peoples come and go—
religion, and government,
   and the wonder of a show.

High is the throne of the priest
   and the titles writ thereon;
wise is the learning there
   that the toiling soul may con;
God spoke in Sinai—
   this also Caiaphas saith;
wherefore the crowd draw near
   because he gives them faith.

High is Pilatus' throne
   with the lictors round about,
to guard the city ways
   where the folk go in and out;
peace upon earth he gives,
   commerce, and all increase,
and the people praise his name
   for that he gives them peace.

High is the throne of the king,
   king Herod that seeks delight,
with conjurers, dancing-girls,
   cupbearers, and men of might:

>   wherefore the people praise
>   his glory and come to see
>   all that the king can do,
>   because he gives them glee.
>   Love is come up for trial
>   before the thrones of the world;
>   where the ancient trumpets sound
>   and the banners dance unfurled.
>   Hear what those governors say—
>   hear how he answers them,
>   in the depth of your hearts to-day
>   as once in Jerusalem.

CAIAPHAS

Thou, Love, that hast made thyself of a worth unpriced,
make answer and say—Art thou the very Christ?

LOVE

Yea, also thou shalt see the Son of Man
coming with clouds of glory; in his van
wonder, behind him fierceness of delight—
I am I and Love is God; thou hast said right.

CAIAPHAS

What need we any further testimony,
for ye yourselves have heard his blasphemy!
He hath made himself God above all man's company
of dreams and visions—wherefore he ought to die.
Religion will not have him—bear him away
to Pilate that he may die this very day.

PILATE

Art thou the King of the Jews?

LOVE

    Thou sayest it.

PILATE

Knowest thou not what judges here against thee sit?
Nor what they tell against thee, witnessing
thou hast published thyself abroad for God and King?
What art thou?

LOVE

   Nay, if my kingdom were from hence
should not my servants fight in my defence?
But neither it is of this world nor they.

PILATE

Art thou a king then?

LOVE

    Even as I hear thee say.
Therefore I came into this world to bear
great witness unto great truth everywhere,
and greatly they that are of truth rejoice
knowing me, seeing me, hearing my voice.
I, Love, am truth's sole witness.

PILATE

      What is truth?
and what is love but a little piteous ruth?
O Caiaphas, whence is this Love brought to me?

CAIAPHAS

Surely he comes from Herod's tetrarchy,
the place of the flesh and fleshly lust and pride.

Part II   THE RITE OF THE PASSION

PILATE

By the flesh therefore let this love be tried,
and crown him or despoil him at his whim.
Bear him to Herod, that he may question him.

HEROD

Art thou that prophet we have heard of then so long?
Art thou that god, cunning and swift and strong,
who is king of the earth and all the heavens above?
Show us some pleasant miracle now, lord Love!
[Silence]
Some wonder of beauty, some loveliness again
thrilling the sense of nerves and exquisite brain;
let us be drunk with a fiery marvel of lust
saving our limbs from weariness and disgust.
[Silence]
Thou prophet, thou Love, that I may set thee free
work thou to-day a new desire in me,
by a magical knowledge show me a golden thing
made apt to delight me in my banqueting.
[Silence]
Wilt thou not? nay then, Love may die for me;
bear him back, soldiers, to his death—but ye,
joyous companions, come, for the hall is lit
and the wine is poured that we may drink of it.

PILATE

Even now I find in him no fault at all;
but ye, O folk, shall bid what shall befall.
O people of all the world! O Time and Space!
O ye who looked on Love in any place,
it is said before me that Love ought to die.
Behold the man!

ALL
Crucify! crucify!

PILATE
Shall I not scourge him and then let him go?

CAIAPHAS
If thou release him thou art Caesar's foe.
Hath not this talkative fellow in each town
sought ever to turn the whole world upside down?

PILATE
I am innocent of his blood; take heed, O priest:
shall I not loose him to you at your feast?

CAIAPHAS
On us and on our children be his blood.
Our house and our tradition he withstood.
He hath blasphemed our God, and he shall die.

PILATE
Even take him now, ye men, and crucify!

MARY
O Son, in a dark hour we bid good-bye.
Seven times as deep as any former pain
I feel the withdrawn steel pierce me again!

LOVE
O lady, what is that to thee and me,
seeing long since we knew these things should be?
for other sheep I have, not of this fold:
them also must I bring, out of night's cold

and hell's. But thou, my other self, content
these children, grievous in abandonment.
Lest mortal love in his dark hour have none
to strengthen him, mother, behold thy son,
dwell with him, cherish him. O mortal brother,
take to thy house thy charge; behold thy mother.

CAIAPHAS
This was thy son who rode upon an ass
to prove himself the god he dreamed he was,
but now can bring no mighty work to pass!

PETER
I fought till all the rest forsook him; say
no word that can me to their wrath betray.
No good can come of serving him to-day.

PILATE
Mourn, soul of man, for never shall our kind
a fairer or a falser vision find
than him whom now anguish and death shall bind.

JAMES
Come, woman; though destruction hide his brow,
and Love be God no more, yet canst thou sew
and cook for who in poverty lie low.

HEROD
Is this then she who bore this man and bred,
pleased that her love shall see at last his head
crowned, and him laid to-night in a soft bed?

JUDAS
Whether he die or reign I must with fire
tormented be, whom with all these his choir,
woman, he long hath racked with vain desire.

JOHN
Hearest thou not what all these witness? Thou
art all of Love is left unto us now.
Yet in my heart there is a house for thee.
MARY
God, God, why hast thou thus forsaken me? (3)

PART III
THE HERALD
Draw near, O people, let us crown our lord.
    Wherewith? With jewelled circlet or with thorn;
   let him, by knees as in his praise or scorn
bent, be with honour or reproach adored.
Let chain of gold or malefactor's cord
    bind round the mortal purple he hath worn:
   let him with outcry to his throne be borne;
for him be wine or vinegar outpoured.

God is he: hearken! this accusing tale
shall for his pain and ending best avail,
    in whose death-filmed eye breaks Deity.
Man is he: think not any thrusting spine
shall less be sharp for power supposed divine,
    or present darkness less for light to be.

Anguish of soul: bound in each bruised limb
    and manacled by tired feet, Love must go
   unto the Pavement, must with curse and blow
be pressed by the fear-ridden Sanhedrim.
Then from fierce hands and hate and faces grim
    shall he be barred by soldiery, that know
   naught but his name, with ordered spear-shafts. Lo,
hard on one side, the Devil, tempting him!

Part III THE RITE OF THE PASSION

Anguish of body: bared to popular eyes
 and popular lips that mouth it and are fed;
last brute deforcement of the mysteries
 wherein the holy flesh is perfected,
the scourging at the pillar, and the flies
 that hum around the breast and bloody head.

O look no more for his descent. No more,
 while the crowd threatens and the priests despise,
 cry out upon him, but with mournful eyes
loosen his body. Lo now, he who bore
our sorrows, our infirmities, and wore
 our weakness as a garment, now Love dies.
 This man desires him and this man denies;
but who of all his people shall adore?

Call no more on him to descend; with myrrh
 anoint him, and remembering how he died
 keep yourselves yet for three days purified
with fasting: watch beside his sepulchre.
 We know not; surely Love may rise again,
 who on the cross of all men's hearts is slain.

SATAN

O Gabriel!

GABRIEL

O thou adversary!

SATAN

See,
can even the power of godhead slip from me?
Shall I not now destroy man utterly?
Look where the world comes out to see him die!

GABRIEL
Also yet more than this may they espy,
ere this hour ends, and thou perchance and I.

SATAN
Look where he stumbles already and falls down,
beneath the mockery of the roaring town,
striking again the head that wears the crown.

GABRIEL
See where the Cyrenean bears his cross;
and the women follow him in his hour of loss.

SATAN
See, where the sticks and spears about him toss!
as he goes up along the Dolorous Way,
and the Dolorous Strokes fall on him day by day.

GABRIEL
See, how Veronica wipes the sweat away.

SATAN
See, how they come now to the place of a skull,
where dry bones are the flowers that men may cull.

GABRIEL
The storm of voices empties in a lull.

SATAN
The sound of hammers is here the only sound:
why do the legions of angels wait around?
is there no help in any angel found?

GABRIEL
Veil, veil your eyes, O armies! height in height
from the youngest princeling seraph to the might
of Michael burning topmost, veil your sight!

Part III THE RITE OF THE PASSION

be nothing at all about him any more
but an abandoned love; till all is o'er
do and say nothing, but adore, adore!
Neither how this is nor what this is ye know,
so far above you and so far below:
I only now to the last duty go.
I who did once before the Maiden move,
now to each heart that would itself approve
proclaim the tidings of the death of Love.
This is the moment when the world is riven
with the exalted mystery of heaven—
Nothing is given until all is given.
In his temptation and his agony
ye ministered beside him; now let be,
there is nothing at all to aid him now but he.
All ministration, all approach, is o'er,
question not, see not, move not; but outpour
in him your angelhood. Adore, adore.
For Love in his great hour must be alone.

SATAN
The work goes on; Gabriel, the work goes on.

GABRIEL
Do thou thy part then until all is known.

Father, forgive them, for they know not what they do.

SATAN
This is my part: from either end of time,
  and from the coiled antipodes of space,
from the first life that issued from the slime
  to the last life that falls away from grace,

I gather up the hosts of infamy,
    I loose the sevenfold mysteries of hell
that in the last encounter ye may see
    if love shall vanquish them or shall dispel.
I summon those who deal in chains and swords,
    affliction wilfully done upon love,
the torturers and evil-visaged lords
    who are most swift to make an end thereof.
Yea, come ye, all you people, to my side;
who is there by whose sin Love hath not died?

GABRIEL

From the last life that still can say *I am*
    being not yet made utterly one with Love,
to the least life that dare not wholly damn
    motions of Love that still within it move,
I call you; all his children, all his folk
    that have for Love's sake suffered any pain,
or known the ache beneath the dolorous stroke,
    come hither and see if that were but in vain;
come to the unfolding mysteries of heaven,
    the transmutations of the body of Christ,
the seven miracles of the Way, the seven
    witnessing words of Love self-sacrificed.
Yea, come ye, all you people, to my side;
who is there that for Love's sake hath not died?

LOVE

Who is there that will follow where I go?
    This is the first slow step upon the Way—
possess within you all that works you woe,
    put off all anger with it and all dismay.

Part III   THE RITE OF THE PASSION

O you at once the slayers yet the slain,
  you friends yet executioners of Love,
know by the anguish of your hearts' own pain
  how ye are guilty of the death thereof.
Come then with pardon, which is the bright speed
  I make to turn each foeman to a friend,
which is the mere refusal to give heed
  to aught but expectation of the End:
I cry aloud in God for them and you—
Forgive them, for they know not what they do.

      Woman, behold thy son.

SATAN

Look, look upon the world! where is the light
  that lately shone upon the streets and skies?
The common day returns, no longer bright
  with heavenly presence and divine surprise.
The common tenderness, the common care,
  can they, O dupes of Love, can they be he?
your earth's devices, that so many share,
  can they be lures to immortality?
O no, the royal dynasty and house
  whereto ye pledged your fealty now is lost;
be brave then, with your sight throw off your vows,
  and buy no fantasy at so great a cost!
This is not Love—that dream is quite undone—
this is but your mother, this is but your son,

GABRIEL

Who will be gentle, blithe, and debonair
  even when the miracle is wholly ceased?
who will make courtesy his daily care,
  whether he serve the greatest or the least?

who will attend his cousins with goodwill,
    even though his own heart faint for need thereof?
though duteous kindness be his only skill
    who late was vassal and blood-brother to Love?
Watch for Love's coming—but in others' need;
    ravage not the wide wilderness for a sign,
but in your nearest neighbourhood give heed
    to what least light may on those neighbours shine.
All else is Love's—this only must be given—
a gate, a place, an opening meet for heaven.

LOVE

Who is there that will follow where I go?
    This is the second step upon the Way—
to know I am born everywhere; to know
    the Child with the Mother doth not wholly stay.
There is no mother but is mother of me;
    Yea, though ye see not ye shall well believe
'tis I whereby at all ye do agree,
    and I whom in all loves ye must receive.
I have given the mystery of my coming-forth
    into the hands of lovers and of friends,
and happy he who there adores my worth:
    who adores me allwhere till creation ends.
I cry, while the world's cycles slowly run,
Son, lo thy mother! mother, lo thy son!
    To-day shalt thou be with me in Paradise.

SATAN

Ye who have stolen love by many a plea
    from others your companions; who have bound
the master of love and master of liberty,
    because in freedom only Love is found;

Part III   THE RITE OF THE PASSION

 ye who have claimed love as your proper due,
  setting yourselves as governors over him;
 ye who have busily begun to sue
  for love to ease an ache or please a whim—
 ye who have brought him into bondage so,
  now when ye find yourselves on a like cross,
 and, he unable to save you from your woe,
  clamour against his wounding and your loss,
 in the good man's claim, the foul man's lechery,
 cry out *Come down* in a common mockery.

GABRIEL

Who is there, O Love, that hath not done amiss,
 seeking to steal and seize and own the grace,
claiming of right some long-accustomed kiss,
 panting with greed of some new-visioned face,
but if they turn—see where they turn and run,
 my company and thine, dove-canopied Lord—
forget the thefts of Love they all have done,
 remember how they acknowledge their reward.
They stammer on the word *Thy will, not mine;*
 entreating still, with folly for a prayer,
that in thy kingdom thou wilt make them thine,
 yet cast not thou thy penitents to despair.
Robbers no more, they sigh *Remember me;*
show them thy favourable liberty.

LOVE

Ere I descend, ere I put off the last
 holy and sacred knowledge of my power,
ere all my godhead be quite overcast
 and I be fallen to my most bitter hour,

THE RITE OF THE PASSION

I cry in a vision, to all my folk I cry,
   all those I have loved and sojourned with so long,
you publicans and pharisees, who deny
   and who betray, who seize and do me wrong,
who spurn and mock me—yea, if but one word
   be loosed across the abyss to me and say
Ah Lord, remember me; in thy kingdom, Lord,
   in a vision I answer and cry to him *To-day,*
To-day thou shalt be with me in Paradise;—
Ah now, what now, what terror before me lies?

    My God, my God, why hast Thou forsaken me?

SATAN

Now I the Cross am risen with all my power
   to rule the thing I bear; now, you strong thrones,
come and behold how I above him tower,
   and beauty lying beneath me stirs and moans,
come and behold the triumph won through me,
   and have no other fear than that he die
and dying rob you of the perfect glee
   to know that Love is no more God most high;
come, all you who have grudged and scorned and sneered
   and anyways denied or hated Him,
yea, also who have fled from him and feared,
   his soul is fainting and his eyes are dim.
O my people, who amongst you will stand up
and put to his lips the last and bitterest cup?

GABRIEL

This is the time when ye can move no more,
   for the Cross bears you, no more you the Cross;
ye cannot choose now, as ye chose before,

Part III THE RITE OF THE PASSION

    for all the world is mere defeat and loss.
Darkness is o'er you, and about you death,
    and in the darkness only dying Love,
whom ye hear moan but know not what he saith;
    nor can ye, if ye would, at all remove,
for ye are fixed in him as he in you.
    Now even the angels of your pilgrimage
cry to you, saying: 'Shall He make all things new,
    this refuse thrown out from the world's bright stage,
this naked, useless, wounded, frenzied thing,
that cannot heal himself of his suffering?'

LOVE

What now am I who hang 'twixt heaven and earth,
    being made a spectacle and a mockery?
Now even my chosen find me of no worth;
    they that pass by shoot out their tongues at me.
What sorrow is there that is like to mine?
    What pain of lovers like Love's very pain?
Behold, in my hands and feet I bear the sign;
    now even I know that even I am vain.
All that was I is given into the grave,
    part seized by violence, part fled by stealth:
others I saved, myself I cannot save—
    where is my victory? where is my health?
where my salvation? where my deity?
My God, my God, why hast thou forsaken me? (4)

[A long silence]

I thirst.

SATAN

In the taste of all the wells of idleness
    and all the running rivers of industry,

shall there be found no waters that can bless
    the infernal mansions with felicity?
All the adventures of the body, all
    the explorations of the aching mind,
these have found out all drugs ephemeral
    and now there is none left for them to find.
Wide and more wide I wander, and behold
    magic on magic fails to give me peace.
No youthful pirate and no prophet old
    shows me a land wherein my thirst can cease.
All things are tried and all things are accurst:
in a rich land of rivers still I thirst.

GABRIEL

Look on this company, O cherished lord!
    since dawn sprang on their souls they waited here
expecting when perfection should be poured—
    nor have they fled for weariness or fear.
Of the world's potions would they never taste—
    nor ease with seeming Lethe their desire;
here to thy buttery have they made haste,
    and shall thy grace not hear what they require?
O 'tis but thou they wait for! 'tis but thou!
    parched in the fevers and the droughts of Love,
they burn, they anguish, but they keep their vow
    who dreamed at dawn of springtime and the Dove.
Thou only best, and all things else being worst,
except thou give them drink they can but thirst.

LOVE

Out of the vanquished woe I turn again:
    I know you separately, I know you all.
O people of my heart, I feel your pain

come in upon me; now no more a thrall
unto a death beyond the deaths ye know—
  infinity's loss being gathered up in me—
I take your deaths into me; I bestow
  my presence on your infelicity.
Drink, drink, for I am given; do but taste!
  why for the brackish will ye leave the sweet
waters which I to bring you have made haste?
  is not that swiftness marked on hands and feet?
Nay, lies one heart in desert places curst?
still, while he drinks not, still *I thirst, I thirst.*
           It is finished.
              SATAN
It is not yet concluded; O not yet!
  Forbear to come upon us, O thou End!
Though all our hopes till now were overset,
  it may be that some hope shall yet befriend.
It is not finished; there is much to do,
  there is more and more to win and store and hold;
all that we gained is vanished, but who—who—
  can be content while aught is uncontrolled?
Be swifter, O be stronger, you my peers,
  grasp, seize, and ravish: beauty is your prey.
We have scourged her and slain her through these many years
  and shall an end come, and that end to-day?
It is not finished; strike, and strike again—
it cannot be that all things are found vain.

              GABRIEL
It is finished! O what messenger, O what light!
  O hear! O is it silence, is it sound?
Naught can be wrong where all things are most right,

and this but foretells what shall more abound.
Deaf, lame, or blind—lo, the renewal comes:
    and these things are but knowledgeable joy—
be deafened now by that delight which numbs
    almost its own capacity and employ.
Be lame, new heavens so fast about us move:
    be blinded by this glory of delight:
and still love's healing issues out of Love—
    and still we are but on the verge of sight.
All things are old and all things are made new:
Truth—O most perfect marvel—is found true.

LOVE
Now with a great voice I begin to cry:
    I am wholly now and utterly come to pass,
ended and perfect is my ministry—
    I am the reflecting and burning sea of glass
imaging that wherewith I must be one.
    Beyond creation that within me lies,
O Love, am I not also found thy Son?
    Creation knows me in how many a guise,
but we are nothing save our Unity,
    which though awhile I was not, yet I was,
and am again most wholly come to be,
    the burning and reflecting sea of glass
which nowise can be dimmed now nor diminished;
lo now I cry with a great voice *It is finished.*

Father, into Thy hands I commend my spirit.

SATAN
They fail, they fail, they are dropping through nothingness,
    they are altogether falling into naught!
O Love, that thou mayst all creation bless,

these too to thy last precipice have I brought.
They that have had Desire for god so long
   feel a Desire much greater than their own;
a stronger power than theirs engulfs the strong;
   all that they showed to others they now are shown.
All that have followed the fire and not the light
   are lost in darkness of a roaring fire,
wherefrom the smoke of their torment to the height
   of benediction does no less aspire.
Since only through such change they reach the End,
into thy hands their spirits I commend.

GABRIEL

There is nothing more to be or do but thou!
   I loose these souls to thee; be thou their soul;
they watched for thee a little moment—now
   take and transform them, O thou perfect Whole.
Even now what rapture in the last long sigh
   impels them into that profound abyss
which is thyself, O God, O Love most high!
   Thou hast made them at first for nothing else but this.
Look, how they fall into thee, and are gone,
   where separation is not any more,
for all in thee are mightily made one
   where thou dost all their proper selves restore.
Hark, how each sighs, finding the perfect end,
Into thy hands my spirit I commend.

LOVE

Even I that am God, even I that alone am heaven,
   will keep the word that is its only law—
Nothing is given until all is given;
   I will make my City whole and without flaw.

Being risen throughout my being I take thee last,
    O tender flesh that wast with me so long,
bear this withdrawal till the hour be past
    and in myself I make thee newly strong.
Except, O pleasant dust, thou undergo
    the operation and high art of death,
how in thy own degree canst thou too show
    what now through all but thee my wisdom saith?
My Earth, that thou mayst in the Unity end,
say: *To thy hands my spirit I commend.*

GABRIEL

Out of the abyss life flows to earth again—
but the suspended ritual waits the slain.
The victory yet is dark, the victor dumb.
Ye officers of his entombment, come;
ye who are left, forlorn and desolate,
approach; undo the fastenings of his fate,
lift him with gentleness into the new tomb—
none, none before have entered in the gloom,
nor have ye yet, despairing, understood
the chill of the body, the congealing blood.
With yet-pierced hearts accept him and remove;
'tis love that waits upon the death of Love.
But ye, angelic armies, from the night
burn with fine rapture through the depth and height,
and cry, in adoration still renewed,
while lightly his entire beatitude
begins to ravage and to empty hell,
Praise to the Name who doeth all things well. (5)

PART IV

THE HERALD

Lament, O world! Love dies and let him die;
   bring him with ritual to his sepulchre,
nor let, to be a deep perpetual sigh,
     Time new-embalm his memory with myrrh:
       [All the Persons] *Love dies and let him die—*
Order the great procession; let all come,
but let their longings and their mouths be dumb.

Inter him with consideration; he
   was once a prince of a most royal house.
Bear him not slovenly or treacherously
   as those would do who have forgot their vows—
     Love dies and let him die—
nor in some plague-pit as an outcast fling;
though he was cast out he was yet a king.

He was the master of all households; he
   went forth with many lovers day by day;
in many friendships was his deity
   exalted in sweet joyous interplay.
     Love dies and let him die—
He hath wholly passed from knowledge and from place,
leaving our poor lives vacant of all grace,

All the fair glances, all the changing eyes,
   all intermingled clasp of hand with hand,
all adoration, all superb surprise
   that did about the things of earth expand—
     Love dies and let him die—
all salutations that can ever be
of such import, of such repute, as he;

all conversation, all instruction, fades,
    they were but ghosts that glimmered at his side,
and if he pass into the place of shades
    how should they any longer here abide?
        Love dies and let him die—
all knowledge passes and all song must cease;
death makes a solitude and calls it peace.

The slow civility of cities now
    breaks up within itself, and is no more;
the most of all delight is but to know
    there is something we a little less abhor—
        Love dies, and let him die—
a little less abhor than all the rest;
we are but quietly weary at our best.

Weary is Pilate in the Judgement Hall,
    and weary is the thought of Caiaphas,
weary is Herod though he vainly call
    for some new revel to be brought to pass—
        Love dies and let him die—
and the poor folk of each Jerusalem
are grown too weary even to strive with them.

Beauty is perishing in a doleful plight;
    and, beauty vanished, what more can we say
than in the morning *Would that it were night!*
    and in the evening *Would that it were day!*—
        Love dies and let him die—
we cannot aid him, we cannot restore,
nor can we bid him rule us any more.

Part IV   THE RITE OF THE PASSION

Beauty is dying because Love is dead,
   and Love is dead! Love, our fair lord, hath died!
Vain were the bloody drops his anguish shed;
   we have no governor and we have no guide—
     Love dies and let him die—
all sweet conclusion is with him destroyed;
there is nothing now within us but the void.

He was a fiery and most powerful god
   and is trampled underfoot as a spent torch!
how vainly to his portals have ye trod!
   there is no temple now beyond the porch.
     Love dies and let him die—
His tabernacles are forsaken: come,
children of men, be tearless and be dumb.

     [A Funeral March]

     FIRST MINSTREL

When the strong son of David
   held all things in his reign,
spirits and kings and peoples,
   he murmured *All is vain*.

When the divine Alexander
   looked over Ganges afar,
he found the weariness mighty
   in all his host of war.

When the great Julius carried
   Rome on his single breath
they asked him what end was fitting
   and he answered *Sudden death*.

When the wise Cicero brooded
   on the purple and the thorn
he said, *Though death be a good gift
   it is better not to be born.*

When the most tender Virgil
   smote on the subtle strings,
this was the music that issued:
   the tears in mortal things.

When the proud English poet
   numbered his hours of glee
he sighed a single knowledge—
   It is better not to be.

Yea, all our wisest utter
   to-day one prayer of pain—
*The roads are filled with darkness;
   let us not live again.*

For hope is dead within us
   and the hope of hope is sped;
who shall be strong to harrow hell
   unless one rose from the dead?

     SECOND MINSTREL

In a place of shades unknown
under a shadowy throne
the shades of men are blown
   after a dying dream;
no gospel there is heard
nor spoken any word,
only the shades are stirred
   by things that only seem.

THE RITE OF THE PASSION

For there each shade beholds
a vaporous cloud that folds
the shadowy throne and moulds
   likeness of its own face;
each over all sees naught
but his own imaged thought
into possession brought
   and having sovereign place.

Natheless, each yet is blown
with sad, inaudible moan
far from that cloudy throne
   and that which seems thereon;
wherefore continually
a flame begins to be
'twixt that which seems to see
   and that which it doth con.

A pale flame wakes and moves
and 'twixt those shadows roves,
which their pained dream approves
   for a perpetual fire;
and still their weary wings
labouring through cloudy things
feel the desire that stings
   and cannot end desire.

From flame to cloud they go,
and cloud and flame are so
that those shades nothing know
   except their own sad will;

for all dreams that abound
of all rich sight and sound
nothing is ever found,
   and nothing ever still.

Wherefore continually
is a great mystery
of things that cannot be
   and visions ever fled;
and how at all should they
find any rest or stay
or dawn of a true day
   unless one rose from the dead?

THIRD MINSTREL

When our Lord came riding
   through the midst of them,
the children ran and shouted
   in Jerusalem,
throwing down their palm-leaves,
   throwing up their caps;
all the babies crowed to him
   from their mother's laps.

When our Lord came swiftly
   through the place of shades,
all the children thronged to him
   fresh from Herod's blades;
the sad dusk was full of them
   whom he did retrieve,
and first the smallest of them all
   from the lap of Eve.

THE RITE OF THE PASSION

Socrates and Caesar
   though he met with there,
though he went a thousand miles
   to the bottom of hell-stair,
yet he came again to them
   when, turning from their play,
all those little Jewish souls
   observed the Sabbath day.

But within the garden
   he slept in double ward;
armed still and silent
   watched the Roman guard;
watched the high prince Michael
   astonished and aware
of a new thing moving
   as dawn filled the air.

And within the chamber
   he slept in single ward;
all the rock was conscious
   of the heavenly guard.
From the air within the air
   a soft wind came,
and above the silent head
   burned the tongues of flame.

FOURTH MINSTREL

Who is this that cometh
   as a wind from the south?
who is this that moveth
   with a song in his mouth?

who is this that laugheth
   since naught goes amiss?
who is this that sigheth
   as for pure bliss?

who is this that bloweth
   and the vapours flee?
who is this that signeth
   and the sick are filled with glee?
who is this that watcheth
   lest a sparrow fall?
who is this that meeteth
   with his friends in his hall?

This is Love in loveliness,
   this is Love in light;
this is Love that singeth
   of a tender sight;
of an old man happy,
   or a young man gay,
or a single dragon-fly
   in its blest array;

of two lovers meeting,
   or of rising birds,
or of a high minstrelsy
   mingling notes and words,
or of all sweet knowledge,
   all sweet thought above:
who is this that cometh?
   children, this is Love.

FIFTH MINSTREL

What great Apostle,
    When the Christ rose,
met with him secretly
    in the garden close?
fast ran Saint Peter,
    fast ran Saint John,
when they heard the rumour,
    but our lord was gone.
Only in the morning
    he was earliest seen
by a weeping spirit,
    Mary Magdalene.

Oft in a glory
    to my heart he came,
only-begotten,
    with love for his name;
but what bitter passion
    on myself for tree
hath his bounty suffered!
    now deep in me,
silent, unmanifest,
    hiding his power,
during a time and times,
    waits he his hour.

High imaginations,
    wait, sad and still,
till a sudden rumour
    your desire fulfil.

> But, O blessed Magdalene,
> when the first dawn
> shines across my spirit
> from that garden lawn,
> watch with me, speak with me,
> blind me with tears,
> when angels fall silent
> and himself appears.

SATAN

There is a thing that man may never do,
    a mountain that his feet may never tread;
the mightiest power is snapped: bear witness, you,
    children of our Lord Love, that he is dead.

Dead in your hearts the Love that lit you lies;
    ye know that he shall never rise again.
Though you shall watch for ever with sad eyes
    your whole lives' grievous vigils are in vain.

Hear ye the word which is creation die,
    the Tree of Life is withered all and hoar;
in that dark separation which is I
    Love fails from Love and shall be God no more.

Through all of Being to the bounds thereof
    I search if aught of it may yet remain.

LOVE

Amen.

SATAN

O Voice, who art thou?

Part IV   THE RITE OF THE PASSION

LOVE

I am Love,
And from destruction I arise again.

[A triumphal March]

LOVE

Now is the world unto its centre come
  and lo I am in its centre: O my few,
my strong, my loved ones, be no longer dumb,
  cry, cry aloud: *Who is on my side, who?*

I am crowned and mitred, I am king and priest;
  I swear by myself I will make all things new,
I in dyed garments coming from the east;
  cry, cry aloud: *Who is on my side, who?*

Fiery and fragrant am I come again:
  of all the deaths and martyrdoms ye rue
there is no moment that at all is vain;
  cry, cry aloud: *Who is on my side, who?*

I am Love, I am Love; I am risen everywhere,
  I am Love in all the hearts that turn thereto;
I in all fairness am the only Fair;
  cry, cry aloud: *Who is on my side, who?*

Who hath kept the vigil, and I did not see?
  who hath suffered the agony, and I never knew?
I am come upon them all with victory;
  cry, cry aloud: *Who is on my side, who?*

Ye who have watched one hour, behold, it ends!
  and I who end it am called Faithful and True;
I have made you free for I have made you friends;
  cry, cry aloud: *Who is on my side, who?*

Also my foes shall find in me their end;
   Caiaphas shall be lit with my new fire,
Pilate shall have a god to be his friend,
   and Herod shall desire man's last desire.

Out of the broken hearts in desert and den
   I hear the cry that lifts to Christendom:
Lo, I come quickly—
        [All the Persons]
                  Even so, amen,
master and lord; even so, Lord Jesus, come.

CAIAPHAS

Wide were my eyes and yet I could not see;
   albeit I taught religion to all folk.
   I could not hear nor tell Love when he spoke.
O Love, fair Love, sweet Love, remember me.

PETER

Fearful of death and reckless cruelty,
   I, who confessed that Love was God most high,
   did with great oaths refuse him and deny;
O Love, fair Love, sweet Love, remember me.

PILATE

I feared the toppling of Rome's royalty,
   and many poor men breaking up my peace,
   wherefore I would not that Love should increase.
O Love, fair Love, sweet Love, remember me.

JAMES

I, who beheld when on the mountain he
   was glorified and did with prophets talk,
   fled lest I should on this last journey walk.
O Love, fair Love, sweet Love, remember me.

Part IV THE RITE OF THE PASSION

HEROD

I sought the furthest pleasures that might be
  and would have miracles wrought in my sight;
  wherefore I knew not Love nor his delight:
O Love, fair Love, sweet Love, remember me.

JOHN

I who received a charge beneath the Tree
  have kept a shelter for the innocent heart,
  making desire a holy thing apart;
O Love, fair Love, sweet Love, remember me.

JUDAS

I fell into a foolish treachery
  exchanging Love for a quick worldly gain,
  whereby he dwells in peace and I in pain;
O Love, fair Love, sweet Love, remember me.

MARY

O Child, I have waited long and watched for thee,
  and all that ever can be said or done
  beneath the sky, all that is lost or won—

LOVE

O lady, what is that to thee and me?
  Even but a ceremony and a sign
that what thy will asked mine hath brought to be:
  didst not thou cry to me: They have no wine?

I have given them wine for ever: yea, in me
  all these are known and I in them am known—
I am the Sole-Begotten of Destiny,
  I am the way; I, Love, am God alone.

I am the close of all men's mortal dying,
   I am living in them as I for them was dead,
I am the defiling and the purifying,
   I am the union, riven or perfected.

There is none on earth that can have place beside me
   nor any of all the angels that is God;
there is none can know what mysteries betide me
   who am those mysteries and their period.

I am the Passion and the Crucifixion;
   I am the Silence and the Rising again;
both far extremes of joy and dereliction
   I draw to myself, and they make answer again.

Say, what art thou, my angel Satan?

SATAN

                                Lord,
   I am thy shadow, only known as hell
where any linger from thy sweet accord.

LOVE

   Say, what art thou, my angel Gabriel?

GABRIEL

Lord, I am nothing but thy annunciation;
   thy message and thy summons, and thy call,
the Gospel to all men of thy great salvation.

LOVE

   And I alone am utterly all in all. (6)

Part IV   THE RITE OF THE PASSION

THE LAST SALUTATION

Let there be set no name to this but one
written by God's finger evermore upon
a white, a shining, an immaculate stone;

yea, if there be amongst you here one power
who hath drunk the dregs of a most bitter hour
and found the oil grown dry, the wine grown sour;

and hath not failed, nor washed from off its brow
the bloody sigil of its grievous vow,
and hath said still: *Yea, also this is Thou:*

praise be to Love for the most happy grace
that still hath kept it in its steadfast place,
praise for the dolour and glory of its face:

praise for the ever-old and ever-new
beauty that shines thereover and therethrough;
and bring us also, O Jesus Christ, thereto. (7)

---

1. Holy, Holy, Holy; Lord God Almighty
2. The Heavenly Word, proceeding forth
3. At the cross her station keeping
4. Throned upon the awful Tree
5. Praise to the Holiest in the height
6. Hail to the Lord's Anointed
7. Praise, my soul, the King of Heaven

TALIESSIN'S SONG OF THE SETTING OF GALAHAD IN THE KING'S BED

THROUGH the palace the torches go;
   who follows there?
Camelot, Caerleon, London, Dover, Verulam,
   and Winchester.
All the cities of Logres come;
all the cities of Christendom.
Up the stairway the torches go;
   who there is gone?
Camelot, Lutetia, Ravenna, Alexandria,
   Byzantion;
even New Rome, even the sacred Crown,
even the immortal central town.
To the chamber the torches go;
   who goes with them?
Camelot, Eleusis, Mona, Hieropolis,
   Hierusalem.
All the priesthoods in order come,
and the priesthood of Christendom.
Into the chamber the kings-at-arms
   royally pour;
Camelot Engated, Dragon Seat, Excalibur,
   heralds before.
All the bishops and princes see
the end of priesthood and royalty.
Round the chamber the knights-at-arms
   stand, a strong line;
Camelot embattled, the noble princes sevenscore,
   the great king's design.
They who now, their armour shed,
bear the prince to King Arthur's bed.

o

TALIESSIN'S SONG OF THE SETTING OF

Into the chamber the great king comes
    and the great queen;
Galahad, in strength more than mighty towns of
    Christendom,
    paces between:
lovely, lovely in his power
as the king's throne, as the queen's bower.

Into the chamber the high prince comes;
    who on him tends,
Galahad, Rose of Gold, Fire of Lilies, Galahad?
    Singers his friends,
Taliessin and Percivale,
undo the buckling of his mail.

In the chamber the high prince turns,
    louting full low;
Galahad King Arthur's hand kisses and Queen Guinevere's,
    Lancelot's also.
To the lords and champions he
bows himself for courtesy.

Over the chamber a silence falls,
    for our lord prays;
Galahad, shining bud of victory, Prince Galahad,
    the Youngest of Days;
time now back from time is come;
to peace the Peace of Christendom.

To the high bed Sir Lancelot's hand
    aids him ascend,
Galahad, Helayne's delight, lilied son of Lancelot;
    King Arthur's friend;
gaze ye all, ye can but see
mystery, mystery.

GALAHAD IN THE KING'S BED

Galahad lies in King Arthur's bed;
   torches depart;
Camelot, Caerleon, London, Dover, Verulam
   have here their heart.
Darkness on the chamber falls,
and the watchmen keep the walls.

From their stations the watchmen call,
   as the night goes,
call through darkness *Galahad*, counter-call *Prince Galahad:*
   deep in repose
sleeps, the Mercy through him shed,
the high prince in King Arthur's bed.

EPILOGUE IN SOMERSET: A SONG OF THE MYTHS

[For ANNE, DIANA, JEAN, and MARY: made at their request]

ABOVE the rippling rivers, amid the swelling combes,
in gardens fair and flowered, in low and lovely rooms,
among the farms of Somerset, the sheep herds and the smiths,
we walked by sun and starlight, and looked upon the myths.

As in a place of mystery, Love's Hierusalem,
the holy sites are gathered, and watchful over them
a Mount of sacred olives looks out on sacred rooms,
so a wonder of great courtesy stood up among the combes.

Within an English garden, below a beechen height,
the lilies grow in summer, and the souls that are as white,
the souls that are as lilies; and where barbarous people strove
we walked with sudden laughter, and made music out of love.

Beneath a common patronage, within a common grace,
we heard the supernatural sounds breathed far through time and place;
in a secluded summer we saw the flaming crowns
of all the antique legends come riding o'er the downs.

Among the spears and scimitars, between the peacock fans,
we saw the Orient glory whose name is Suleiman's,
and by the Great King's bridle the Sheban wisdom glowed,
outside an English window, upon an English road.

EPILOGUE IN SOMERSET

Beside an English gateway, within an English porch,
the words of great antiquity arose as lamp or torch,
the aureoles of the casual names that yet can sound so high
their subtle invocation brings the gods of vision nigh.

A voice went calling by me, and ere the voice had died
I saw among the swelling combes Diana all enskied,
Diana of the Romans, Diana of the night,
the buskined maids about her, the hunting javelins bright.

A voice went calling by me, and ere the voice had ceased
the mother of the mother of God ascended from the east;
I saw the vigil ended, and the light of Israel come
where Saint Anne stood up to prophesy the tale of
   Christendom.

A voice went calling by me, and ere the voice was done
rose up our lady Mary, deep vestured with the sun,
a vision of two thousand years, a tower of mighty crowns,
one foot among the ships at sea and one among the towns.

A voice went calling by me, and ere the voice had stayed
came streaming o'er the wooded hills the banners of the
   Maid,
Jeanne and her company of peers within the fiery dark,
the myth of mortal valour that went heavenward from
   Arc.

I heard my own voice calling, and lo above the springs
the princess Michal walked in peace, between the striving
   kings;
calling a name of childhood—the gate of heaven's own
   hall
in the prince Michael opened, a flame angelical.

EPILOGUE IN SOMERSET

O fast and thick about us the dreadful myths went by;
they thronged the combes of Somerset, they thronged the
 English sky,
the legends of antiquity, the everlasting forms
who are lamps amid the darkness and torches in the
 storms.

And by those mortal courtesies invited and ensouled
I saw my Mantuan Duchess, a darkness turned to gold,
where unadorned among them she lifted up her head,
touched by the work alchemical, in union perfected.

In unconcluded verse I named the heavenly Mount of
 Rome,
the hill of Saint John Lateran, whence shining thoughts
 have come
on Augustinian errand all the Saxon thanes must con;
I named the names of splendour—elect Byzantion;

the queen Iseult of Cornwall, with Tristram at command;
the queen Morgause of Orkney, with Lamoracke at hand;
King Arthur and Lord Lancelot, and crimson in his mail,
serving the last Achievement, the Master of the Grail.

O song amid the rivers! O laughter 'mid the combes!
O wonder in the gardens and beauty in the rooms!
O myth on myth arising, and cast among them thus
the crying of the sacred word the Sunday sang to us:

'He shall not let that Holy Thing which is abroad on
 earth
fail from the house of friendship, the place of joy and
 mirth;
by all the myths and legends, by the tale of Christendom,
He shall not let His Holy One into corruption come'.

EPILOGUE IN SOMERSET

The night is on the rivers; the night is on the combes;
a dozen lights are shining in far-divided rooms;
but deep within the firmament, high over sun and star,
where the great myths dwell for ever, the days of Aisholt are.

AISHOLT,
    by permission of GOD and OLIVE WILLIS,
        August 1930

www.ingramcontent.com/pod-product-compliance
Lightning Source LLC
Chambersburg PA
CBHW062026220426
43662CB00010B/1498